It is through woman that ideality is born into the world and what were man without her There is many a man who has become a genius through a woman, many a one a hero, many a one a poet, many a one even a saint, but he did not become a genius through the woman he married, for through her he only became a privy councillor. He did not become a hero through the woman he married, for through her he only became a general. He did not become a poet through the woman he married, for through her he only became a father. He did not become a saint through the woman he married, for he did not marry, and would have married but one, the one whom he did not marry, just as the others became a genius, became a hero, became a poet through the help of the woman they did not marry - Soren Kierkegaard

Part 1

Sitting there at my desk, resting my head upon my fist, I continued my usual classroom pastime of admiring my watch. Its gold Arabic numerals are set against a faded white face, and the bronze hour and minute hands are tarnished just the right amount to give it a distinguished aged look, but my favorite part is the bright red second hand that smoothly and continuously sweeps over it all to the quietly delightful sound of ticking.

My watch is my prized possession - a 1961 Tudor Oyster I had set into a comfortable black leather strap as a present to myself for my highschool graduation. Its moderately-sized round face and dull silver casing stands in stark contrast to the large and garish stainless steel bracelets worn by the other, more brutish, men in the Iowa State College of Business.

I began to wonder how much time was left until class was dismissed, so I reached for the iPhone in my back pocket to check the time. With seven minutes to go, I turned my attention to the short and pudgy man (if he is even worthy of being called a man) standing at the front of the room. His orange button down shirt was wrinkled as if it had been balled up on the floor before he put it on, and the poor guy was already balding by his mid twenties.

He continued speaking. "I have two masters degrees. One in communications science and the other in philosophy of religion, so you can all be assured that I am more than qualified to be your TA for Speech Communication 212. I promise to grade you all fairly and impartially - unless you try to give a speech that Star Wars is better than Star Trek! Ha! Ha!" He laughed nervously.

Christ, I thought. *He desperately wants us to like him.*

He went on."If you apply yourself and listen to what I have to teach you, I will show each and every one of you how to become effective public speakers."

I looked around to the other students in the classroom. No one was paying him the slightest bit of attention. My mind began to drift off as well.

I thought about Reanne. I was meeting her for coffee in twenty minutes, and I needed a chance to smoke before I engaged with her or I would be fidgety and decidedly unattractive. When the TA declared the class officially over, I was already at the door reaching for the pack of cigarettes in my front right pocket. I made a mental note not to return to Speech Communication 212 until it was time for me to give a speech, lit my cigarette, and purchased an album on my phone that had been recommended to me by Apple. Apparently, they have some sort of algorithm that analyzes taste in music and makes a suggestion individually tailored to each user.

You, my dear reader, may be wondering why I buy my albums from iTunes when I could be using Spotify for free. You have to understand, my dear reader, that Spotify being free to use is precisely the reason I do not use it. I put on my black Ray-Ban Wayfarers and purple Beats wireless headphones by Dre (they match my cell phone case) and began listening to my new minimalist electronic album as I made my way across the smoke-free campus to meet Reanne for coffee.

My name is Christopher Duncan. If you are reading this because you expect me to tell you who I am, I'm afraid I will disappoint you because I do not have a clear answer to that question myself. The best I could possibly do for you is give you the label that other people usually employ to describe me "antisocial". The term is far too simple for my own taste. It entirely betrays the superficial and oversocialized worldview employed by normal people where anyone who smiles is good and anyone who doesn't is bad solely because they make unpleasant company.

As to my own self-perception, it runs much deeper than that and there are infinitely many more conceptual frameworks I could use. I could speak to you in terms of the natural sciences and explain that obsessive-compulsive, borderline, hypersexual, and schizotypal tendencies are the result of a disinhibited central nervous system caused by a hypoactive prefrontal cortex. Likewise, I could take an aesthetic approach and identify myself with Heathcliff, Gatsby, Meursault, and Stephen Dedalus. I could even describe myself to you in religious terms. When I first noticed that my ring finger was significantly longer than my index finger, indicating high prenatal exposure to androgens, I immediately thought of Psalm 51:5. *Behold! For I was evil in the womb and in sin did my mother conceive me.* As you can see, my inner subjectivity is so rich and expansive that I could go on forever in this manner, but for the sake of brevity I will instead elect to give you some cursory, objective facts before I arrive at the coffee shop where I will meet Reanne.

The most important thing to know is that I am adopted. Twenty years ago I was born to a (supposedly) devoutly Catholic girl who found herself pregnant at the age of fourteen. After the required twelve days in a foster home I was adopted by Tom and Jeannie Duncan, a couple as stable and not unconforming as any other members of the Iowan upper middle class. As far as adoptive parents go I have no complaints, but through no fault of their own I could not help but feel as though they did not love me unconditionally like the other parents did with their children, and please, my dear reader, don't give me all that crap about how I should feel "chosen" and "special. Adoption is hardly any parent's first choice, and for those of them that it is, the idea of saving a poor helpless unwanted baby seems so good and selfless that they can't help but reek of self-righteousness. A while ago I read a study that adoptive parents spend more money on their children than average, but spend less time with them. It makes sense. They act in accordance with their "good parent heuristic", but nevertheless, the oxytocin which is released during the act of childbirth and responsible for that endless maternal warmth is absent. Consequently, at the core of my emotional life there is a sense of being foreign, of being not quite like everyone else, of being eternally alone, and despite what others may think, I spend my time in isolation, not because of a misanthropic nature, but because I am not entirely sure what makes people seek out human companionship in the first place.

In addition to my adoption, there are two other qualities that set me apart from other people. The first is my intelligence. I would describe myself as a genius if it wasn't impolite to do so. My mind is always racing, but it is of little consequence since I rarely think of anything other than myself, and you most likely wouldn't notice it anyhow. I usually keep very quiet, and you would undoubtedly pay more attention to my appearance. No, I am not implying you, my dear reader, to be shallow by any means, but it is human nature to seek out pleasant stimuli and many people find my face gives them considerable pleasure. The simple truth is that I was blessed with extraordinarily good looks. I do not mean to say that I am ordinary run-of-the-mill handsome, but rather that I possess a rarer form of androgynous beauty that appeals to males and females alike. I am precisely six foot with a perfectly sculpted one hundred sixty pound body, and I have thick, brownish-blonde hair which I carefully tousle to drape over my bright blue eyes. Girls are drawn to my strong brow and sharply defined jawline while, at the same time, I frequently catch men admiring my long eyelashes, full lips, and small snub nose turned up just enough at the end to give all the charm of an aristocrat without the offense of snobbery.

Furthermore, my image is enhanced with a wardrobe of black v-neck t shirts, dark purple sweaters, tight faded blue corduroys, and a black leather belt (with a rectangular stainless steel buckle) to perfectly match my black leather industrial boots with yellow laces - I polish them daily. When it gets colder I will add my black bomber jacket and gray scarf with vertical olive green stripes. I only wear a backpack on the weekends. It is unfashionable to wear one during the week because it makes you look like you actually care about school.

I arrived at the campus coffeeshop five minutes before I was supposed to meet Reanne. Twenty minutes later I received a text message that "she had got caught up in something and could we please reschedule for two hours in the future." I sent her back that it was ok.

On my way out of the shop I heard a bubbly female voice say "Hi Christopher!" I turned around and was face to face with Liz standing far too close to me for ordinary conversation. This was known to be a habit of hers and was by no means limited to me. She immediately went off on what class she was headed to and God knows what other irrelevant pieces of trivia she felt compelled to share with me. I asked her if she would like to stop by my apartment after class was over. She said yes and skipped away, singing a song to herself as she did. She was wearing one of those plaid jumpers like the girls at my Catholic elementary school used to wear. Though I wouldn't ever want to be seen with her in public, I had always suspected Liz of being a good fuck.

When it came time to meet Reanne again, I thought it would be best if I showed up ten minutes past when we were scheduled to meet. I still ended up waiting twenty minutes for that bitch. She finally arrived, and I was struck by not only how differently she looked but also how differently she carried herself. I hadn't seen her since December (it was August now). She had elected to take a semester studying abroad in Greece. Why she chose Greece when she studied French as her major I never bothered to ask, but the answer she would have given me most certainly wouldn't have been the truth at any rate. Presumably she just finds men with a Mediterranean complexion more attractive than Northern Europeans.

As far as looks go she wasn't really anything special. She was tall for a girl (my own height), but skinny and her height was primarily attributable to her long legs. Additionally, she had rather masculine and severe facial features; undoubtedly her body produced a large amount of testosterone for a woman (her hands were chronically dry and much larger than my own). It really wasn't her looks that I found attractive, however, but her personality - strange as it is to hear a man say such a thing.

I recognized right away on our first date that she scored very highly on the Hare psychopathy checklist. The way she smirked and said "And now you know my deepest, darkest secret." after telling me her middle name made it clear that she did, in fact, have plenty of secrets hidden deep within her thoroughly dark soul. I remember thinking it sounded like something I would say.

My eyes met Reanne's. She never looked down or broke eye contact like any of the other girls in my life. We ordered our drinks and had sat down facing each other before she began to speak. She started by telling me about the Bible camp she counseled at over the summer. She is an Evangelical, you see, of the kind whose mind is a never-ending stream of fantastical and self-righteous religious zeal.

I've never had much respect for Evangelicalism. At least Mass offers a solemn space to contemplate your wretched and sinful nature. I expect Reanne is on too much of a "Jesus High" during a Christian rock concert to ever consider how much her concupiscence has displeased God the Father. I read that prayer, especially when it is self-righteous in nature and performed with the social reinforcement of other adherents, actually activates the pleasure circuitry in the brain in the same way that drugs do. It made sense in Reanne's case; she was definitely a pleasure seeker.

I say this because Reanne was clearly one of those girls who will proudly declare her virginity for all to hear, but if you dare to inquire how many dicks she's sucked or how many times she's taken it up the ass, she will icily respond that "we all make mistakes, but luckily Jesus' crucifixion wipes us all clean" (of course it is always said without even the slightest hint of remorse in her voice).

Usually on dates, I make a point to let the girl do most of the talking - things just seem to work out better that way, but with Reanne I hardly ever said anything at all. She never listened anyway, but at this point she saw fit to take advantage of her highly developed social skills to turn the conversation back to me.

"What was it you were studying again?"

I told her, "Physics and Finance."

"And why did you choose that particular combination?" She asked.

I gave her the usual spiel:

"Finance is the second highest employer of physics grads after research. It all has to do with the application of differential equations."

It made me sick to speak as if my course of study was a well thought out plan. Truthfully, I hated both majors. Physics was boring and so far removed from ordinary life it might as well have been fairies and dwarves I was studying rather than electrons and neutrinos. The only reason I stuck with it was because name, gpa, and major were printed in the local newspaper at the end of each semester, and I couldn't stomach the idea of some prick I went to highschool with seeing I switched majors and thinking *I knew that arrogant twat wasn't nearly as smart as he thought he was.* Finance, by contrast, was exciting but I was drawn to it entirely for the same reason I was fond of craps, and at this point in the story I had already lost several thousand dollars on coal futures. It disgusted me.

Reanne and I continued our conversation for about an hour though in reality we just spent the time eye fucking each other. She had great style, I had to admit, and everything she wore came from Goodwill of all places. Oh, how I wanted to get underneath that black button down shirt with pink floral print to those perky, triangular breasts.

Reanne left first. She had a meeting for the campus ministry exec board, which was convenient because at this point I was boiling with rage and concealing my anger required all of my effort and focused attention.

While I didn't listen to much she had to say, I couldn't help but hear the part about the British man she met in Greece. She even said it hurt her feelings that he never wrote to her, the stupid cunt.
I intended to write her a letter while she was away, you see, and towards that end I had spent two weeks practicing Spencerian script so that the letter would be beautiful. She never gave me her address, and so I wasn't so much upset that she had had a fling but that she had never had a chance to admire my handwriting.

Still I hated her and I hated this British man, whomever he was. She even mentioned that the guy was an atheist. He probably even subscribed to all that quasi-spiritual garbage about how the universe was beautiful and filled with wonder. I could just picture him, some insufferable pseudo intellectual, a hipster too no doubt, a unique special snowflake just like all the others.

My anger continued to build on the way back to my apartment, though you wouldn't have been able to tell if you passed me by. Most people get loud and expressive when they're mad. Not me - I get quiet, completely silent and stone faced. My thoughts become too loud to interact with the outside world and I become trapped within the confines of my own mind. I couldn't stop thinking that Reanne was a stupid cunt and how could I let a dirty whore humiliate me like that? I smoked three cigarettes on the way to my car - a 2006 Black Buick Lucerne with leather interior. It was Tom's old car, but all of the dents were mine. I hooked up my iPhone to the auxiliary port and put on Pretty Hate Machine for the 347th time (my cell phone keeps track) and went for a drive to take my mind off of Reanne. My car redlines at 107 miles per hour.

While I was driving I couldn't stop thinking about how much Reanne had changed since the last time I saw her. She used to have hair that went down to the middle of her back and she acted the part of a sweet and innocent girl who had spent her life riding horses on her grandparents' farm.

Now her hair was cut shoulder length and she carried her pride openly displayed in the way she walked, over arching her back like she knew how much I wanted to fuck her but was so self satisfied by her knowledge that she would never allow that to happen.

I thought back to when I had confessed my love for her, right before she left. A stupid move on my part to be sure, but you have to understand how drunk I was at the time with the idea of marrying her. Dreaming of all I could accomplish with her as my wife and accomplice (and of course how intense the sex would be), I told her I would wait for her - the most idiotic move imaginable.

Though I do not normally act emotionally, when girls are concerned I often feel so strongly that I am inclined towards making a complete and utter fool of myself. She coolly replied that she was "in a period of growth and not likely to commit to any one person any time soon."

I was furious, but I couldn't stop thinking about her. I even had to delete my Facebook account to keep from spending all of my time staring at her photos, but even that wasn't enough because on more than one occasion I couldn't handle the mystery so I secretly reactivated it in the middle of the night to check up on her. Every picture that had another guy in it made me so jealous I'd end up throwing an empty beer bottle at the wall.

But still, for all the torment Reanne caused me I couldn't really blame her for any sort of moral failing. Most people think love is some sort of noble and selfless experience of transcendence, but it isn't like that at all - It's a game whose rules are governed by the physical differences between the sexes in their quest for reproduction.

If the girl gets fucked she loses

If the man falls in love he loses

It all goes back, you see, to the way we evolved in the wilderness thousands of years ago. It was advantageous to the females if they could get a man to be emotionally attached in order to protect and provide for them and their offspring. Likewise it was advantageous to the males if they could impregnate as many girls as possible without sticking around to raise the kids.

For this reason (though I doubt she's conscious of it) I'm sure Reanne enjoys telling men "I'm sorry if I led you on in anyway" as much as I enjoy telling girls " I didn't mean to imply I was interested in anything more than sex."

By the time I returned to my apartment it was dark and I had essentially calmed down. After smoking two more cigarettes and taking another shower (3rd for the day) I saw that I had a message from Reanne on my phone.

It was really nice catching up with you today. I had a lot of fun. See you again soon. :)

I panicked. Perhaps I've been misjudging Reanne this whole time? Maybe she really is the sweet and innocent girl other people think she is. But could all of my previous observations have been wrong? I was unsure, but I didn't care. I loved her. She was perfect. I wanted to be with her forever.

I began to pour out my heart in response, to fling myself at her knees so to speak, but I stopped myself halfway through and hesitated. Doubtlessly Reanne was watching the text bubbles on her screen and eagerly anticipating my response (which would have signified her victory had I sent it), but instead I thought back to Amanda and the advice she had given me the summer before last.

I worked with Amanda at a small local store. She was an older middle-aged woman, but rather attractive for her age. Her massive breasts and the way she always wore a shawl over them gave her a benevolently maternal appearance, and I quickly became close with her. She was blonde haired, blue eyed, and promiscuous, just as I had always pictured my own mother to be. She was always telling me how handsome I was and that she was sure I was going to grow into a ladies' man just like her son.

Needlessly to say, we ended up in bed by the end of the summer, giving us both the pleasure of incest without breaking any actual taboo.

I laid there with my face nuzzled between her massive breasts and for the first and only time in my life I felt like someone was taking care of me, and I felt like I was safe. I told her so. She was silent for a long time, but then she told me "If you ever like a girl, never tell her. It takes away all the mystery." She didn't say anything else and I haven't seen her since. Utilizing her advice, I deleted my half-written response and decided I would not text Reanne back at all.

I remembered reading a study that showed how women are predisposed to cheat on their partner when they are ovulating so that their offspring carries alpha male genes. If I had to choose between being the beta male that Reanne cheats on or the alpha male she cheats with, I'd choose the latter every time. I can't imagine anything more humiliating than getting cheated on.

I tried to sleep but I just saw Reanne when I closed my eyes. It got me all worked up considering how upset I was with her for trying to manipulate me like that. In order to try to take my mind off her, I rolled a joint and went over to the disk golf course across the street to smoke it. I had smoked marijuana many times before, but this time was different.

I usually enjoyed getting high - the brighter colors, and enhanced textures gave life a sensory depth that made me realize how dull life ordinarily appeared. It always reminded me of reading the Chronicles of Narnia with Jeannie when I was boy. At the end of the series the characters die and are reborn in a world that's identical in every way except it's more vivid. That's how I interpreted getting high.

Most people who smoke marijuana do it as a social activity and they put on a movie and have conversations. I don't understand how they do it. When I get high I become too engaged in my own sensory perception to follow a plot or interact with people. Besides, I can't really stand all the people who think they're "enlightened" just because they do psychedelics.

One time I walked over to the Subway near campus and ordered a sandwich. Ordinarily a sandwich just tastes like a sandwich, but this time I could make out all the individual tastes and how they perfectly blended together. It was an almost spiritual experience - the bread as the base with the savory turkey, white American cheese, and tomatoes filling out the middle, all topped off with the sweetness of honey mustard. It was the most pleasurable experience of my life.

I ordered two more sandwiches and it occurred to me why there were so many fat people around campus. I don't usually eat much (it's kind of a chore actually), but if eating always felt that good I would be fat too. I was even scared that I would end up eating my fingers.

This time wasn't like that. I became so inwardly sensitive and aware that it was pure torture. My eyeballs scratched as they rolled around in their sockets. I felt every drop of mucus flowing down my throat. I felt the leverage on my vertebre and I thought that I was going to snap in two. I couldn't bear it.

All I wanted was to stop feeling. I drank gin and mineral water until I passed out. I awoke the next morning late in the afternoon on the floor covered in my own vomit. I had to throw out my black v-neck which didn't bother me too much since I had four more just like it.

The next thing I did was flush the rest of my marijuana down the toilet. I had just bought it a few days earlier and there was nearly an entire eighth. Thinking back I wish I had sold it, but I was too shaken up to think straight.

After I showered and cleaned myself up, I walked over to the forest near my apartment. It's a fairly large wooded area with the sort of rolling hills that are rare in Iowa. The entrance is through a small graveyard which gives the whole place a kind of otherworldly feel to it. The paths aren't maintained either so my boots are always muddy when I leave. It doesn't bother me since the mud washes right off, but I imagine it appears strange to the other students. In fact, I'm pretty sure it adds to my image - that I'm about to shoot up the school or something. As far away from the truth as that is, it doesn't bother me that they think that. At least they notice me - it's the invisible guys they should really be concerned about.

A ways into the forest there is a shoddy wooden bridge that crosses a shallow stream. It's a remarkable piece of construction considering how warped it is - the planks are at nearly a forty-five degree angle. I sat there on the edge of the bridge for a few hours, my mind completely blank.

Eventually a group of three guys came by and sat next to me. While I always avoided interacting with other people on campus, I didn't mind meeting people in the forest. Something about seeing other people there made me feel like we were kindred spirits.

On campus people were always asking what your major was and bragging about the "research" they did with a faculty member or the prestigious internship they had lined up for the summer. I couldn't stand talking to those sorts of people. How they can live with themselves kissing ass for the privilege of mindlessly entering data into Exel or getting coffee is entirely beyond my comprehension.

The guys were little better than average looking, but I could tell they weren't all that concerned with their appearances. They were wearing all different colors of Vans with dark raw denim jeans and wore plaid flannel shirts. One even had a thick moustache like you would see on a middle aged police officer.

They asked if I wanted to buy drugs. I declined, but I could tell they were getting defensive so I offered them cigarettes so they would know I was cool. They became comfortable and sat there smoking on the bridge with me. We chatted for a bit about how nice it was to get away from everyone else in the forest. It was Saturday and all the other students were at the football game. One of the guys mentioned how lame they all looked in their red and yellow Iowa State T-shirts and offered everyone another cigarette.

"I tried to get into football," I said "but it always upset me when my team lost.."

We sat there in silence for a while until the guy with the moustache quietly added "It's easier to not care than it is to care and be disappointed."

We all agreed and looked down at the water. No one said much of anything after that.

When it was beginning to get dark, they asked if I wanted to head back to their apartment. They had just pooled their money to buy a vaporizer and they assured me that it was amazing how smooth the hits were. I politely declined and told them to take care. They were noticeably disappointed, but they thanked me for the cigarettes and went on their way. After the previous night, I had no intention of smoking marijuana any time soon, and besides, I was much too physically attractive to hang out with them.

On the way back to my apartment I checked my phone and noticed I had a message from Reanne asking if I had any plans for the night. Of course I never did, but I never wanted anyone else to know that.

I sent her a reply that I was hanging out with another girl I had just met. Obviously it wasn't true, but I wanted her to think that it was. At any rate, it was certainly a believable lie. It's funny. Back in highschool when I was skinny with bad acne and terrible posture I desperately wanted a girlfriend, but now that I can walk around campus and get smiles from a dozen new girls a day I never really bother to ask any of them out.

I went back to my apartment to get something to eat. I fried up three eggs and some ham (my usual dinner) and ate it while listening to Rachmaninov's second piano concerto. I could never get enough of that piece. The deep rolling of the strings always made me feel powerful which is something I desperately needed at the moment, because I couldn't stop looking at my phone to see if Reanne had replied. She hadn't and at this point I seriously doubted that she would. I was furious. She could have replied with anything and it wouldn't have bothered me, but the fact that she ignored me sent me over the edge. I can't stand being ignored.

After I finished eating and cleaned myself up I put on my sunglasses and walked to the park. There is something very satisfying about wearing sunglasses at night. I've never quite been able to put my finger on exactly why that is, but I would guess that it's just because you aren't supposed to do it.

When I arrived at the park I took my usual spot on the swingset and chain smoked the rest of my cigarettes. There were six or seven left in the pack. There isn't anything pleasurable about smoking that much at once, anyone who smokes can tell you that. In fact, anyone who smokes knows cigarettes are better the more sparingly they are used. Still, it was something to do and I needed something to help me keep my mind off of Reanne.

Christ, I thought, I *probably love her*.

I hated myself for it. She was such a whore. I sat there gently swinging back and forth a long while. I wasn't keeping track of time. My iPhone had died which was shameful since I even had the special case that doubled the battery life, but it wasn't any surprise considering how compulsively I had been checking it for Reanne's response.

Occasionally I looked up at the stars, what little I could see anyway - light pollution I think they call it. Orion was the only constellation I could ever really pick out. I always liked Orion. It really did look like a man with a bow and arrow. The other constellations just looked like lines to me when I looked them up on the internet, but maybe people just had better imaginations back when they were being catalogued.

I thought back to the framed little saying that hung in the living room of Tom and Jeannie's house.

Maybe they aren't stars, but rather holes in the floor of heaven where the light of our loved ones shines through, letting us know that they are happy.

It always annoyed me how sentimental and wishy washy that saying was. It just sounded out of place in an age where everyone knew that the stars were flaming balls of hydrogen. It was as if Jeannie was just choosing to shut off her brain and live in blissful fantasy instead of coming to terms with the vast emptiness of the universe, but I suppose I can't really blame her for that. In fact, I actually wish I knew how she did it.

The sun was coming up by the time I returned to my apartment. I wasn't tired and I doubt I could have fallen asleep even if I wanted to. I fried three eggs and some ham for breakfast, showered, and changed my clothes. It had been about six hours since the last time I had smoked, and my head was beginning to pound so I walked to the convenience store to buy another pack. After that, I returned to my apartment and watched Mad Men on Netflix for the rest of the day. I had already watched the series through a few times, but I didn't care. I couldn't focus. It just felt good to stare at the computer screen and not think about anything.

Several hours later I remembered it was Sunday and it occurred to me that I hadn't lifted yet. Luckily the university gym stays open until midnight. It was a little past 9:30 PM, so I had plenty of time to finish my workout before it closed. It's funny. After you've been lifting for a while missing a session causes a lot more discomfort than making the effort to go. It's the feeling that you're deteriorating. It's unbearable. Besides, I've always found that lifting becomes more enjoyable the worse my mood is. It makes me feel powerful to angrily lift up a barbell and drop it back down.

Becoming strong certainly changed the way other males relate to me. I remember when I first came to Iowa State I always felt like I was in the way of other people. Walking around campus, I was always dodging through the crowd like the other guys would run me over if I didn't watch my step. It isn't like that anymore. Now I have the impression that most of the other guys stay out of my way. Sometimes one will even give me a slight nod as he takes a slight step to the side. It's a nice ego boost.

When I arrived at the gym, I swiped my ID card at the desk and went to the locker room to weigh myself - 159 - I was losing weight. I made a mental note to eat four eggs with ham and cheese when I was finished. After I took a dump (always take a dump before you lift), I walked up the three flights of stairs to the weight room, put my wallet (black leather) and cellphone in the temporary locker, and adjusted the rack.

For me, lifting isn't the chore it is for other people. It gives me time for my mind to wander, and I often do my best thinking when I've got 225 pounds on my shoulders. This time I was thinking about how I got into lifting in the first place. It was a year ago next week. Reanne had just told me that she didn't want to be more than friends because she had too much going on in her life to handle a relationship right now. I knew what that meant - I had blown it. I made a lot of mistakes, but I didn't know better. I didn't get a lot of female attention back then - I was far too nervous and fidgety for that.

Truthfully, the only reason I even had enough confidence to go over and grind on her at the back to school dance I had stumbled into (I had been out walking because I felt lonely (I felt lonely a lot back then)) was because I noticed she pointed me out to her friend.

The next night we went for a walk. She cut out rather early and I could tell the attraction she felt for me at the beginning of the date was completely gone by the end of it. I approached the date like I was trying to prove I was good enough for her which is, not coincidentally, a disastrous mindset for a man to have with a girl. Nevertheless, she had shown me a little attention which was more than enough to cause me to become terribly infatuated with her.

The next day I watched the movie Troy. When I saw what Brad Pitt looked like in that movie I decided to take up lifting. I didn't care if it took a year, all I knew was that I was going to improve myself to the point where I could either have Reanne or break her heart - whichever option suited me in the future.

You, my dear reader, might be wondering why I would choose to embark on such a strange course of action, but you, my dear reader, must understand that considering how obsessive the state of infatuation is for me, there was no choice at all. It was the only course of action I had (although a less conscientious person might have stalked and raped her), and I know for a fact that I'm not the only one who experiences love this way. It's called limerence and it's caused by the same gene that makes people alcoholics..

I remember reading *Diary of the Seducer* by Kierkegaard. Johannes, his alias, mentions that every skill he possessed could trace its origin back to a courtship gone wrong. After one heartbreak he learned French, and after another he developed an aptitude in poetry. I related immensely.

In middle school I was talking to Jessica on the phone. I told her I was nervous for high school. She said she wasn't going to have a pity party for me and hung up the phone. She dumped me the next day. I spent the next month reading *The History of Western Philosophy* by Bertrand Russell.

Ashley and I never even had an amorous relationship. I wasn't popular enough for her, so I just admired her from a distance. I taught myself how to dance, alone in my room.

Amber actually told me I was too smart for her, which is hilarious because these days it seems girls enjoy the fact I know what an erogenous zone is. She's the reason I'm now a campus fashion icon.

Reanne was nothing special, and I knew it - just another name on the list, but still, limerence is painful and you can't really do anything but wait until it passes. Luckily for me it never lasts for more than a year, but it supposedly lasts decades for certain people. I would kill myself if that was my case.

At this point it's worth noting I could have any girls on that list without lifting a finger. It's sad really that girls peak so young and decline so fast. They get to be middle aged and become bitter once they realize that there's a darker side to life that they never experienced because they were showered with attention and adoration when they were younger. It isn't that way for men, thank God. It's all uphill after the teenage years, and having already experienced how hellish life can be when you're at the bottom, it's just that much sweeter when you're at the top.

After I had finished my workout, I smoked a cigarette (smoking is even more pleasurable after you've exerted yourself) and returned to my apartment. I fried four eggs with some ham and cheese and took two big gulps of gin with lime so I could fall asleep. The next day I woke up late in the afternoon, and after finishing my regular morning routine I walked to the university library for some reading material. I checked out Don Juan by

Lord Byron. Reading was more enjoyable if I could insert myself into the story.

I climbed the three flights of stairs to my usual spot on the edge of the balcony overlooking the library's interior. I liked keeping watch over all the people coming and going. To my great displeasure, I found my spot occupied by one of those annoying sorority girls who looked like all the others. I'm sure you, my dear reader, can guess what she was wearing - a mint green windbreaker with black yoga pants (so tight you could see her buttcrack in the middle of her flat ass) and those terribly obnoxious brown Ugg boots. How that style ever caught on is entirely beyond me, but then again it's not like girls have to try all that hard to be fuckable.

I settled for a spot by the window overlooking the parking lot behind the library. There wasn't nearly as much activity going on out there, but at least I could make out my reflection in the glass. It gave me something to rest my eyes upon in between pages.

When I found myself bored with reading, I exited the library intending to head over to the coffee shop for a cappuccino but I noticed there was a large crowd gathered in front of the library. It wasn't unusual. They call it a "free speech zone". I decided to walk over to have a closer look.

In the middle of the circle there was a fat, bald man wearing an all white suit with a red bow-tie. That's correct, my dear reader, a bow-tie. *Fucking Douche*. The man was holding up a Bible and commanding the crowd to repent. It wasn't what he said, however, that I noticed so much as the way he said it. Each sentence was said slowly and deliberately, and he varied the pitch and volume throughout.

"Keeeeep the womeeeeeeeeen (high voice) in their placeeeees (low voice). Reeeeal men (high voice) don't watch cartoooons (low voice)."

To me it sounded so insincere and theatrical I wondered if it was, in fact, satire. As comical as I found his preaching, however, it had a curious effect on the people who were gathered around him in the crowd.

"I can fuck whoever I want!" (sic) some trashy looking girl shouted out, red in the face.

A scrawny kid wearing an anime t-shirt cried out "M-m-my mom's a p-pastor and you're a d-disgrace!" He stuttered the whole way through.

I scanned the faces in the crowd and felt nothing but disgust for the other people I saw there. It isn't proper for anyone to ever be proud of how far they've fallen from the ideal figure of Virtuous Man. Fat girls were taking off their shirts to show the preacher their tattoos and there were ugly men sloppily kissing each other in his face. I couldn't help but to think they were all pathetic - not because they were degenerate (God knows I've done far more "degenerate" things than any of them) but because of how insecure and unstable the preacher's presence made them. It was as if they weren't so much trying to convince him that what they were doing was acceptable, but rather themselves.

As for the preacher, I am entirely sure he's just a hypocrite who gets off on attention. I would bet any amount of money he masturbates to interracial porn the minute he gets home. Still, I had to respect how well he handled the crowd, showing no signs of self doubt, and openly wearing a shit-eating grin that only made the crowd even more hysterical. Doubtlessly I could learn far more about public speaking from him than I could from my TA, even with his masters degree in communications science.

I noticed that a girl had joined the crowd a short while after I did. She was standing slightly behind me and to the left, but so close to me her body was practically pressing up against mine. Eventually she asked me what I thought about it all.

"It's interesting." I said.

She wasn't unattractive so I gave her my address and told her to stop by later. Nothing else eventful happened.

The next day was the semi-annual career fair which was always interesting. Everywhere I went I passed by people wearing oversized and wrinkled suits straight off of the rack from Kohl's. It was like they thought that simply wearing a tie and blazer made them ready for the professional world.

Christ, I thought, *how could they be so unaware?*

They looked like children playing dress up in their father's clothes. I even saw a few of them wearing brown shoes with black belts.

I would be dead before I allowed myself to be seen at the career fair. I couldn't stomach the idea of groveling before the HR reps - the older versions of the sorority girl who stole my spot in the library - pretending to give a shit about their companies.

I attended the career fair only once when it was required of me. I didn't stay long. It annoyed me to have to wait in line just to have a fake conversation with women wearing khaki pants paired with a solid color polo shirt that had the company logo stamped onto the left breast. Besides, I didn't have a resume and it was impossible to compete with the others who had stooped to the level of perfecting the fine art of "resume building".

It wasn't so much that I refused to write a resume out of any sort of principle, but rather that I didn't know what to put down in order to communicate my potential. Tell me, my dear reader, what I could have put down? My academic awards? They aren't impressive considering how many A's professors hand out these days. My fluency with the exceedingly complicated program Microsoft Word? Everyone puts that down. It's a bad joke.

At any rate, without a resume the recruiters just flirted with me, like I was a pretty face without any brains. It frustrated me, but I couldn't blame them. I couldn't just tell them that partial differential equations, a class that many of the brightest students on campus seriously struggled with was as easy for me as tying my shoes. I'd look like a total tool if I did, but so goes the life of a genius.

David Hume said that the way society perceives genius is the same way it perceives the ignorant. They can't understand either. Sixty IQ points in either direction from 100 makes communication altogether impossible and so I left the career fair without anything to show for my effort. It didn't make a bit of difference to me anyway. The whole schtick seemed an awfully lot like an exercise in pantomime. I read that 70% of jobs are filled through personal connections rather than the formal interview process. If I really wanted a job, I figured I would be better off just trying to meet other people but I didn't even care enough to do that. The very idea of ever working for someone else made me sick to my stomach.

I decided I would attend my philosophy class on a whim since I didn't have anything better to do. The class took place in the auditorium of the hog research laboratory, a sign of how overcrowded the campus had become. I took a seat in the back row as I usually did when I decided to attend class. The lecture for the day was on the ethical theory of Utilitarianism which was actually the third time in my college career that it had been presented.

The teacher was a tall and skinny man whose slouching posture made it appear that he was, in fact, lecturing to the floor. He wore a black turtle-neck and thick black glasses over his exceedingly feminine face. I didn't have much respect for him. He even hyphenated his last name with his wife's. *What a pussy.*

As I've gotten older and developed my own thoughts, I've come to despise the academic sort of philosophy that is formally taught at universities. It just doesn't seem like it has any sort of relevance to life in the modern world. The way it posits Man as a rational creature capable of moral judgement just isn't true. Stanley Milgram's obedience experiment had already revealed the truth. People were just animals that acted on bestial impulses and emotions. The vast majority would even kill a man screaming for his life just because they were told to.

But it wasn't just the substance of the lecture that irritated me, but the way he presented it - as if the trolley problem was a great deep paradox that would revolutionize the way us students view the world and make decisions. Clearly he wanted us to look up at him all wide-eyed and proclaim him the bringer of our enlightenment.

Christ, I thought, *what a mediocrity*.

At one point he even gossiped to the class about a colleague who was having an affair with one of his students. He said it all self-righteous, like he was so morally superior, but I knew the truth - he was just envious none of his students wanted to sleep with him.

I, of course, spent my time in class carefully observing my fellow classmates. I could tell they never really got anything out of class either. They were merely content to spend their class time on Facebook until they received their credits at the end of the semester.

It's a shame really. The only branch of philosophy that my classmates could probably relate to, existentialism, is never touched upon at all. The insignificance of modern life was something they were all aware of, if only subconsciously. It's all perfectly summed up in that famous picture:

The Pale Blue Dot. Even the most committed nihilist couldn't come up with an argument that rivals the power of seeing the vast emptiness of space.

Nevertheless I never spoke up. It was unfashionable to be seen participating in class. In fact, the only person who ever did was a small boy with a high pitched voice that caused everyone else to give into a perfectly synchronous and collective eyeroll. He offered his sophomoric opinion, always a restatement of the professor's own belief, from the front row, and he acted the part of a puppy that was returning the thrown ball to his master.

When class had ended, I was returning to my apartment when I crossed paths with Alex, a girl I knew from my previous years spent living in the college dorms. She went by Alexandra when I first met her but had recently decided to go with the more gender neutral Alex around the same time she embraced feminism and decided to sport a short pixie cut hair do.

Alex asked if I wanted to go back to her apartment and smoke some marijuana. I agreed, since I knew she was actually asking for sex. While we were walking, Alex filled the silence by explaining to me, in detail, all of her recent sexual exploits and her experimentation with cocaine. Though it never bothered me what a girl's sexual history was, there was something supremely unattractive about her saying it out loud. I began to lose interest, but I continued with her since I didn't really have anything better to do and made a mental note to wear a condom.

When we had arrived at her apartment she took me to her room and tried to kiss me. It's strange, kissing is absolutely disgusting unless romantic feelings are involved - then it becomes even more pleasurable than sex. I thought about how much I wanted to kiss Reanne which made me angry so I pulled Alex's hair and pushed her onto the bed just because I could. I told her to blow me which upset her.

"It's like you only view me as a sexual object." she whined

I found her positively repulsive at that point.

"You're not even good for that." I replied and walked out the door.

I read a study that women who take birth control become less attractive because it changes their hormones and makes them act less womanly. I think that's what happened with Alex.

She came after me, sobbing uncontrollably and I was overcome with a feeling of pity for her and regret for how badly I had treated her. I returned to the bed and let her rest her head on my chest. I laid there for a few hours stroking her back which was not entirely unpleasant, I have to admit.

Eventually I grew hungry and Alex offered to cook dinner for me but she didn't have any eggs or ham so I returned to my own apartment.

While I was walking, I passed right by Reanne. I almost missed her completely because I was trying to light a cigarette (the day was exceptionally windy). I know it was her. I could just barely make out her face right as she quickened her step to get past me. Her face was bright red. In fact, I was actually a bit frightened - I had never seen a woman look that angry before. It must have upset her that my sunglasses made it impossible for her to know whether or not I had noticed her.

It was a nice ego boost to know I had such an effect on Reanne's emotional state. Smirking to myself, I began to lust after Reanne. I quickly became frustrated, however, since I knew she wouldn't ever allow herself to be in a situation that might lead to consummation - she was too aware of her own value as a woman and how much that value would go down once she lost her virginity.

Still, I couldn't stop thinking about how great the sex would be especially considering how much we presently hated each other. It's funny really, how empty and mechanical sex is without emotion - it's just a race to orgasm - but add emotion, especially hate, and the whole experience takes on a life of it's own.

Even though I knew she would refuse, I decided to try my luck, even if just to see how she would respond. That's what kept me fascinated with Reanne. I couldn't ever tell whether she meant what she said or was just toying back with me.

I sent her a text message.

Are you sure you don't want to come over and have hate sex? Your voice is so attractive I'd love to hear what you sound like when you moan.

For twenty minutes I eagerly anticipated her reply. When it came I was not disappointed.

I know what I want, but it is waging war within my soul. I choose Jesus - not you.

I was dizzy. Only Reanne could compose a rejection that implied she wanted me badly, thereby fanning the flames of my own desire. Still, the other implication enraged me. I didn't like the idea that I was being passed over for somebody else. I couldn't stand playing second fiddle to anyone - even Jesus.

I replied feigning indifference.

See you around campus sometime. Take care of yourself.

She did not respond after that.

The rest of the week was torture. I desperately wanted to contact her, but I would not dare ever give her the upper hand again after the way she abandoned me while she was in Greece.

It's funny actually, the way romance works on a modern university campus. Everyone knows the person who cares the least has the most power, so courtship becomes a war of wills over who can hold out from contacting the other person longer. It's sad in a way, how counter intuitive it is.

Especially when you think about those love poems and letters people used to write to their sweethearts. Try anything like that now and you'll be labeled clingy and weird.

Consequently there were few actual couples on campus. The few there were were ugly people who were just lucky enough to find someone else to give them attention. The beautiful people just played games with each other until the initial rush wore off and then moved on to someone else. I was cynical, yes, but only because I knew true love was possible. I knew a couple in their early sixties, a regular old Darby and Joan. They married at 19 and have hardly ever been out of each other's sight since. They even work together during the day. Yes, love was possible, but it had to happen young before people get too experienced. With every new partner love becomes just a bit more blasè like you've seen it and done it all before.

Reanne was my last chance to have what that couple had. I started to feel melancholy, because I knew it was already too late for us, but then I remembered the couple were just codependents anyway and the feeling quickly passed.

Still, I nevertheless enjoyed our current situation. You, my dear reader, may be thinking that what Reanne and I had was toxic and unhealthy. I concede that it probably was. We certainly didn't trust each other at all. But you have to understand, my dear reader, that even when romance is bad it's still a great deal more fun than the boredom and drudgery of ordinary life. Yes, Reanne made me *feel,* and through all of the ups and downs I at least understood why people would speak in those sentimental clichès about how "Love will change the world" and all that. Of course it is utterly ridiculous to speak like that (love is just vasopressin and oxytocin) but I could see how someone less intelligent might think that it was something more.

The rest of the week passed by slowly. I thought about Reanne constantly - from the moment I woke up in the morning to the moment I finally was able to fall asleep. I stopped attending class completely.

Although I never attended class much previously, I had at least always done the minimum amount of work necessary to keep up my grades. Now I didn't even bother with that - it just seemed so pointless.

I wanted Reanne so badly that it physically hurt in my chest. I guess that's why they call it heartbreak.

I did nothing productive and the amount of cigarettes I smoked doubled. I smoked nearly a pack a day. I was trying to condition myself to crave nicotine instead of Reanne; I at least had the power to reward myself with cigarettes. I spent my time wandering aimlessly around campus hoping to pass her by. Often I thought I saw her in the distance, and the palpitations of my own heart would shake my own perception. On closer inspection I was always mistaken. There were an awful lot of girls on campus with blonde hair and long legs.

With the weekend approaching, I resolved to find something to amuse myself with. There was a football game on Saturday so I thought I would go walk amongst the tailgaters before the game. I liked crowds. There was always something interesting happening somewhere and of course there would be plenty of female attention.

Apparently back in Victorian England mental hospitals employed prostitutes to cure men of "lovesickness". I thought that was hilarious. It was true, I just needed to find a new girl and, of course, as soon as I forgot about Reanne or she happened to see me talking to another girl, she would desperately be trying once more to win my affection.

On the day of the game I dressed myself in my tightest blackest v-neck in order to show off my muscles and I made my way over to the football stadium about three hours before the game started. I caught my reflection in the window of a building as I walked by and admired how good I looked. I had taken special care to shave exactly two days prior so I had the perfect amount of stubble for the occasion.

When I arrived at the stadium, I noticed that it was much more crowded than usual. I had forgotten that this weekend was the annual Iowa vs Iowa State game. RV's were everywhere and people were packed together nearly shoulder to shoulder in a sea of yellow and red t-shirts. I weaved through the crowd and amused myself by playing a sort of chicken with the other guys who crossed my path. Whoever stepped aside first lost - bonus points if they apologized. I always won, but I suppose it was unfair considering how much wearing black made me stand out. God help me if I was ugly.

I helped myself to some food that was on a plastic table. It had been a while since I ate potato salad, or anything else besides eggs and ham for that matter.

When the game was forty-five minutes away from starting, I began to make my way back to my apartment, taking great pleasure in walking the opposite direction of the flow of the crowd. I saw Reanne up ahead. With our present courses we would pass right by each other.

I noticed she was talking with a rather wimpy looking guy that was following one step behind her and to the right, someone she had met at the Christian club no doubt.

Reanne and I made eye contact She looked down, and right as the corners of her mouth turned upwards to form a smile, the pain in my chest was not only lifted, but replaced by an overflowing sensation of pleasure in the back of my head - like I could actually feel the dopamine rushing through the reward circuitry of my brain.

I had never felt anything like that; I'd call it ecstasy. I wanted more.

I don't know if the guy was perceptive enough to catch the moment Reanne and I shared, but I hoped he was. I liked the idea of completely humiliating him. I composed a text message to Reanne.

Admit the other guys in your life are boring and I will take you back.

She immediately responded.

What other guys?

It upset me that she would think I was so stupid - I had just seen her with someone. Even if they weren't involved, there were surely others.

I remembered reading a study that showed how someone's commitment to a relationship was inversely correlated to the number of quality alternatives that person had. That's the problem with college campuses. With 30,000 people all in their sexual prime there was always others to choose from.

I replied.

There is always other guys.

The next response was the one that set my life moving in a new direction.

Christopher, I can't do this anymore.

I stared at my phone for a long time. Did she compose it pridefully as if I was nothing or in pain with tears in her eyes? It made all the difference as to how I would respond, but there was no way way for me to know for sure from just a text message. I just stared at my phone, paralyzed by my own uncertainty.

I spent the rest of the day in bed completely overwhelmed by my rapidly vacillating emotions.

On the one hand she was a truly malicious woman and I hated her for all that she had put me through. On the other she was a sweet and innocent girl whom I had deeply wronged. My perception switched back and forth, each lasting no more than a few seconds at a time.

Eventually the fear of losing Reanne for good built up within me to the point of anxiety. I could bear it no longer. I composed a rather long message apologizing and asking to see her (It's embarassing looking back but the words just gushed out of me, like vomit). When I tried to send the text I received an error message and I gathered she had blocked my number.

I read once that the fear of being alone is one of the most common fears people have; It's right up there with the fear of death and the fear of public speaking. I thought it was funny at the time because I'm alone so much and I didn't see what there was to be afraid about. At that moment I knew. I was hysterical with the knowledge of my complete and utter isolation.

I rushed out of my apartment, desperate to just see somebody, anybody, but there was no one around and nowhere to go so I wound up in the large open field of central campus scanning my surroundings for any sign of life. I didn't even see a squirrel.

I looked up at the sky and tried to find Orion, but the sky was cloudy and not even a single star was visible. I fell onto my knees, and as I began to cry I pushed my face into the cold ground.

Part 2

The next two weeks were a blur. I just wasn't there mentally. I spent my time wandering aimlessly around campus.

I knew I wouldn't be returning to Iowa State once the semester was over. Even if I decided to catch up on my coursework and manage to pass my classes with C's, I would still lose my scholarship. It seemed arbitrary in a way. I thought to myself that the hardest thing about graduating from college wasn't the work, but rather going four straight years without ever realizing how pointless it all was. It didn't seem worthwhile to have to borrow money to continue my "education."

I was under a lot of stress, but not because I was bothered by the prospect of flunking out. I was stressed out because for the first time I did not have the luxury of knowing where I would be for the next two years. It forced me to think about my future.

I hated thinking about it. Every time a Boomer asked what I wanted to do with my life I felt sick to my stomach. I disliked Boomers and the patronizingly way they always asked the question. They expected you to answer with a career, as if you had to justify your existence by making a choice between lawyer, doctor, or architect - as if simply living wasn't enough.

Even more annoying, however, were the people my own age who bought into their narrative. I once overheard a classmate say to his friend

"People think college is supposed to be fun. You should work hard and get a good job so that way you can have fun when you retire."

Christ, I thought. *What a jackass. Doesn't he realize he could be dead by 40, never having amounted to anything more than a corporate wage slave?*

I pitied him. He probably even had fifty thousand dollars in debt and had no choice in the matter. Thank God I escaped that fate.

The other extreme, people who gave up and went all Bohemian annoyed me just as much. I knew a couple people like that. They were always dirty - like animals..

I wasn't anything like either of them. In fact, I actually had a great deal of ambition - even if it wasn't really directed at anything in particular. I wanted to make something of myself. I wanted to meet my mother someday and watch her be all sorry for giving me up. I don't care if you, my dear reader, think that was a pathological thing to say. Revenge is just as good of a motivator as anything else.

I thought about what Alexander the Great was doing at my age. He was already raising an army and conquering nations. What would he be doing had he been born in 1995? He'd probably be on the bridge smoking marijuana, if I had to guess.

I knew I'd have to get a job once I left school. I had been coasting by on Tom and Jeannie's dime for far too long. Tom put 200 dollars a month into my checking account (which paid for my gin and cigarettes) and Jeannie even purchased all of my textbooks for me. Every semester she looked up my classes and made sure all the textbooks were delivered by the time I went back to school. I knew it was pathetic to be taken care of like that at my age, but It's not like I would have had the motivation to do it myself. I just straight up didn't care. In fact, the only reason I even went to Iowa State was because it was free on account of my nearly perfect ACT score. It didn't even seem like I had a choice of whether or not to go to college at the time. People just talked like it was a given that I'd graduate high school and go off to college. Of course Jeannie made sure that I had all the forms to fill out. I don't think the applications would have been sent off otherwise.

I thought maybe I would get a job in construction. It would be a good way to toughen myself up a little bit. Of course I could always be a waiter at some fancy restaurant. I'd probably make good tips provided I flirted with all of the middle aged women.

One weekend Alex invited me to a party she was throwing at her apartment. I accepted the invitation welcoming the distraction from my unnerving thoughts, but I wasn't all that enthusiastic about actually attending. I had been to parties on campus before and they were usually pretty lame. There was never even any dancing. People just stood around in groups, four guys to every one girl. Conversations started with "What's your major?" and ended with "Where are you from?"

Still, I bought a fresh bottle of gin and drove over to Alex's apartment. I walked right into her house without knocking and went straight to the kitchen to pour myself a drink. Alex came over and gave me a hug. I pretended like I was glad to see her, and she introduced me to a group of guys who were standing around drinking bottled beer. They all looked like copies of each other.

They were skinny, extremely so, with pasty white skin and patchy beards. Their hair was shaggy and hung over their faces covering up their eyes. They told me they were music majors and that all of them were going to move to Colorado when they graduated.

Christ, I thought. *How unoriginal.*

They were friendly enough until I told them I was majoring in finance (I didn't want to receive incredulous looks by telling them I majored in physics and finance). Presumably they lumped me in with all of the frat guys in the college of business that they resented for being popular and having success with girls or maybe they were just socialists, I don't know, but I felt them become hostile towards me. At that point I left them without saying anything and walked around the apartment looking for a girl to talk to, but there were hardly any girls there. The few there were happened to be ugly.

I sat down in the armchair which was in the corner so I could see everything going on and watched the other people who were in Alex's apartment. After a while it began to make sense to me what had happened. The way the other guys kept glancing over at Alex made it clear to me that she had simply invited guys that were in love with her and taken care to only invite ugly girls so as to have no competition for anyone's attention.

I watched a group of high school kids help themselves to my gin. While I was mildly annoyed, I decided not to do anything about it. They looked so young.

Alex walked over to the group of musicians I had been talking to earlier and led them back to her room. She began making loud and fake sounding sex noises. Presumably she just wanted everyone else to know she was engaging in sexual behavior.

The high schoolers came over and talked to me, but I didn't really enjoy that conversation either. It was like they were trying so hard to act older, and they needed my validation in order to succeed.

I didn't want to be at the party anymore so I drove back to my apartment. I was fairly intoxicated but I didn't have any trouble. As long as you don't drive too recklessly or too cautiously so as to arouse suspicion you'll be ok.

After another week of aimless wandering, I received a text message from Fabian. He asked if I wanted to go to a strip club. I hadn't ever been to a strip club before but I liked the idea of trying something new.

I drove over to Fabian's apartment to pick him up. I knew Fabian from back in high school. He was ugly, but I didn't mind hanging out with him. He had good taste in music and the way he dressed made him look rather tough and intimidating.

Apparently he was in the middle of a fight with his girlfriend. I didn't know much about her, but every time I had been around her she nagged me about smoking cigarettes so I could see why Fabian would want to spend some time away from her.

We had a nice conversation on the way to the club. I mostly just listened to him tell me about the new hip hop album he had found, but it had been several months since I had had a real conversation with somebody else so I was just thankful for the feeling of interpersonal connection.

It was just a little passed 11:00 when we arrived. I parked the car and we walked in together. I felt so giddy I kept tripping over my own feet.

After checking our ID's the bouncer stamped my hand with a bright red skull and crossbones which annoyed me because of how unfashionable it was. I spent the rest of the night hiding my hand inside the sleeve of my bomber jacket (by this point in the story it was comfortably autumn).

Fabian and I took our seats at the stage and we set about rather self-consciously trying to figure out how exactly one was supposed to act at a strip club. Fabian and I watched the girls come out. Truthfully they were a pitiable lot and none of them elicited any sort of attraction in me or from what I could gather the other patrons. They just seemed so worn out all the way from their dry hair to their trashy tattoos. Their eyes were glassy; Their breasts were saggy, and while they "danced", it wasn't to the rhythm of the music. Still, we all just sat there staring at them because that is what you do at a strip club.

Eventually one of the younger and more attractive girls came over and put her arm around me. She was blonde like I preferred and when she whispered into my ear asking if she could give me a private dance I was overcome with the desire to do just that. I would have taken advantage of her offer if I had the money, but I didn't want to borrow money from Fabian for a stripper. That seemed rather humiliating.

She left, but I wished she would have stayed. I followed her with my eyes the rest of the night and felt jealous every time she took another guy back to the private area.

Christ, I thought, *I'm the type of guy who would fall in love with a stripper.*

That's when I decided I wouldn't ever go back. Besides it probably wouldn't even have been interesting once it wasn't new anymore. Most things in life are like that. Sex with a girl was hardly enjoyable after the first time. No cigarette was nearly as pleasurable as the first one I smoked. I bet even sky diving gets old after you've already done it.

I could tell Fabian was very nervous and I wanted to get away from him. I felt kind of bad about leaving him; he looked kind of sad as I walked away, but I needed to be by myself. When people get nervous like that I feel like I'm being smothered and I need room to breath.

I walked up the stairs and leaned up against the railing on the balcony that overlooked the club. There were two boys huddled together on a couch far way from the stage. They were looking down at their shoes. Obviously they had just turned 18 and were anxiously testing out their newly found freedom. Each one was likely wishing he was at home, but convinced the other he was having a good time.

On the opposite side of the club there was an identical couch with a fat old man sprawled out and surrounded by three girls who were treating him as if he was the most handsome man they had seen in their entire life. He was wearing a camouflage baseball cap, and I gathered he was some sort of trucker. I shuddered to think about how much of his paycheck went towards perpetuating the fantasy the girls gave him.

Occasionally there would be a young girl of about eighteen or nineteen that would be pushed up on to the stage by her boyfriend. The way the girls giggled and blushed while they took off their shirts to reveal their nubile young breasts was truly an enjoyable sight. I could tell they were high on both the idea of doing something they weren't supposed to and on the excitement of the novelty of the situation. They stood in stark contrast to the professionals who had seen and done it all before. I had to admit, if the young girls' performances weren't so infrequent, I would probably spend every weekend there.

Eventually, Fabian approached me and told me he was ready to go home. While we were leaving I noticed that the window near the door had been broken and there were several police cars in the parking lot. At that moment I was struck with a sudden sensation of how sleazy the establishment was, and I was disgusted with myself for having spent my Friday night there. I think Fabian felt the same way.

"So what did you think?" He asked me when we were back inside my car.

"I'm glad we went." I replied. "But I don't think I'll ever go back."

"Yeah." Fabian said. "At least it was something to do."

We didn't speak at all on the way back to our apartments.

The next day I woke up late in the afternoon and walked over to the bridge to write some poetry. When I arrived the bridge was gone. There weren't any pieces of it left over or anything. It was as if it had completely vanished. I couldn't help but feel a little lonely as if I had lost a friend. There was something charming about how well it functioned as a bridge even though it was ugly and warped. I tried to capture its significance to me through poetry but I was trying too hard and it just sounded pretentious.

I left shortly after arriving and intended never to return. The area was spoiled for me now. I left upset partly because I wouldn't meet any other people there anymore (even if they just wanted to sell me drugs), but mostly because I would never know why it was gone.

I was overcome with a sudden urge to attend Mass. You, my dear reader, may ask why I would do such a thing. I don't really have a good answer for you. Every now and then I'm just struck by the compulsion to go. I concede that I probably don't seem all that much like the religious type, but you'd be surprised. I've had several profound religious experiences throughout my life. At one point I even wanted to join the priesthood. Of course that was before I hit puberty and discovered women.

One time I was on the bridge and praying the rosary in the middle of the night when I was visited by the virgin Mary.

"Mend your ways and return to Christ." she told me

I was overcome by such a zeal for righteousness that I fell on my knees and wept. I threw off my scientific worldview and took a leap of faith.

God loved me and he had a plan for my life - that's why I was born to a girl too young to raise me properly. All my suffering had a divine purpose. I was the chosen one. God saw all of my sins and He still loved me. I would spend my life serving Him and spend eternity at His side.

Of course the next day I realized it was just a schizotypal delusion caused by the trance-like state I had entered into. Sitting alone in the dark and saying repetitive prayers will do that to you. I thought about how 2000 years ago Saul of Tarsus experienced something similar and it completely altered the trajectory of his life. He had the luxury of taking his experience at face value. I did not. Yes, I believed in God - I just knew he didn't exist.

It was Saturday night and so I walked over to the campus church. It was one of those modernist churches with everyone seated in a circle around the alter. Presumably they were trying to compete with the hip upbeat services the Evangelicals had for the attendance of young people. It wasn't proper for the Catholic church. In fact, much of the pleasure I derived from going to mass dealt with the traditional aesthetic. I liked the sight of stained glass windows that filled the air with colored light. I enjoyed listening to sounds of old hymns echoing throughout spacious chambers. I even liked the smell of incense. Without such sensory stimulation, how could I ever hope to feel like I was holy?

I took a seat in the back row, and while I was contemplating my own depravity, I saw Cassie, an acquaintance of mine walk in. It had been several months since I had last seen her. I had heard that she had recently gotten engaged to her boyfriend Jake.

Cassie noticed me, smiled and walked over. After genuflecting with all of the false piety of someone who had grown up in Catholic school, she took a seat next to me.

"It's good to see you here." She said. "I've come to mass every week and this is the first time I've seen you."

"Every now and then I just get the urge to come. It's inconsistent." I replied.

We were quiet for a while, but then Cassie leaned in and whispered to me.

"Everyone else here is probably wondering who you are. You're not Jake."

"I know." I responded coolly. "You're making me look bad."

She laughed. "No, you're making me look bad."

"Hey," I countered "you're the one who sat next to me."

Cassie blushed and looked coyly down at the ground. "I suppose you're right about that."

At that moment I was struck with such a violent desire to take that girl right then and there. I know she wanted me to, the way she was breathing heavily and all red in the face. She was so feminine in a way that only religious girls are. I spent the entire hour admiring her slender body and the thin white sundress with floral print she wore. My hands shook due to the shear amount of self control I was exerting.

When Mass had ended and the congregation had let out the collective "Thanks be to God." Cassie turned to me and shook my hand before immediately scurrying away. If we weren't in a church I would have fucked her, there was no doubt in my mind. I wondered what the chances of her marriage succeeding were. I hoped it would succeed, I liked Jake. Still, Cassie was quite a bit more attractive than he was and as already evidenced by the previous events, temptation has a way of working itself into the most unlikely of places. I wanted to contact her, but it wouldn't have done any good. She would have just started bragging to everyone who would listen about how creepy I was for making an advance. Of course she'd be rather

pleased with herself at any rate. There's that old truism *men desire women,*
but women desire the desire of men.

I was hungry so I decided to walk a few blocks over to the Chinese
Restaurant I frequented with Fabian. It was a small place, a shack really, but
the owners were always friendly - one of those immigrant families who did
all the work themselves without hiring any help. I ordered my chicken with
plum sauce at the counter, poured myself some hot tea, and took a seat in
the corner booth.

I wondered what would have happened if I had taken Cassie right
there in the church. People probably would have been so shocked they
wouldn't have even known what to do and just stood there watching. I don't
think I would have felt any embarrassment or shame at all. It struck me that
that was precisely what made controlling the impulse so difficult. Ordinary
people would be too terrified of the reaction of others to have that as a
serious temptation. Of course I would have ended up in jail, but I would
have been emotionally indifferent to that outcome too.

As I listened to the food cook just behind the counter I became lost
in my own thoughts. *What exactly was God trying to tell me through my*
experience with Cassie? Was he playing a joke on me? Did I need to make
an act of penance? I resolved to say the rosary after I ate in order to be safe.

I looked forward to it. I really did like praying, but I suppose that all goes back to what I said before about the pleasure circuitry. Still, if you close your eyes and focus on nothing but the rhythm of the words sometimes you lose all sense of self and fall into a blissful trance. It's almost like you've finally experienced something bigger and more important than yourself.

By the time I had returned to my apartment, religion all seemed pretty silly to me so I decided not to say the Rosary after all. As I turned on my laptop to watch Netflix, I thought to myself:

Forgive them Father for they know not what they do; Forgive me Father for I know not what I think.

It seemed rather poetic so I jotted it down in my notebook.

As the weeks went by I continued to spend my time wandering around campus without any direction. I was hardly able to sleep at night no matter how much gin I drank. I thought less about Reanne and more about my future (although she still laid claim to a significant portion of my time). I saw her once while I was walking. She was laughing and talking with another guy. She didn't seem to notice me, but I was inclined to wonder whether she had and consequently exaggerated her enjoyment in order to make me feel jealous. It upset me that I didn't have any definitive way of knowing, and whether or not her motive was there, it certainly worked.

Midterm grades would be published soon and I knew I would have to explain the F's to Tom and Jeannie. Doubtlessly, they would think I was taking drugs. Though I had been clean since I had flushed my stash, I dreaded having to explain myself to them. I would almost rather that they think I was on drugs than know the truth - that I completely lost my mind over Reanne. It's not like they could understand how stressful relationships were for me. The only people who did seem to understand were other adopted people. (I knew a few. It's a very Catholic thing to do after all.)

I resolved to tell Tom and Jeannie that I was taking a break, that I was bored with college and needed to experience something new. It wasn't untrue. I couldn't focus in a lecture to save my life even before I took an interest in drugs and girls. I wouldn't ever reach my potential here at Iowa State anyway, writing papers I didn't care about to be graded by TA's I didn't respect. Yes, I needed to move on to move forward, but I needed to have a plan in order to speak with conviction. If I spoke all timid-like Tom and Jeannie would overpower me and treat me like a failure. The only problem was, I've never really had a plan for anything.

I checked my phone and noticed I had a missed call from my brother. I can't remember whether or not I've mentioned him already. We aren't all that close but we have a lot in common regarding our personalities with the exception that he is much more socially active than I am. He was two years younger than myself, also adopted though from a different set of parents so it's not like we shared any blood or anything. He was currently experiencing his first college semester at the University of Northern Iowa, and I hadn't heard from him in a while.

While he was undoubtedly one of the most original and intelligent people I knew, he had a short attention span and lacked the capacity for memorization that is necessary to receive good grades. Consequently, everyone always thought of him as the dumb one, but that always struck me as rather unfair. He actually had an uncanny ability to zero in on my biggest current insecurity and bring it up in conversation, and although it pissed me off to no end, I was always impressed at his ability to do so.

I thought I would give him a call. He was always enjoyable to talk to even if it did slightly annoy me how much of a faggot he was. Now, I don't fault anyone for having a homosexual experience or two. God knows I've taken it up the ass from my dealer a few times after getting high (though I always regretted it. He had a habit of regressing to some sort of childhood mentality and would cuddle with a teddy bear after I quickly left.) It was the people who made homosexuality their sole identity that annoyed me with the way they spoke with that effeminate lisp so unbecoming to a man. It's like they have no ability to define themselves past their sexual preference.

My brother picked up the phone and we chatted for a while. I was curious to know how his experience at college was. It sounded like he was having a good time and his first semester was much different than mine was. He had quickly become popular.

It's funny, considering how fashionable it is to hate on psychoanalysis in the psychology world these days. According to Freud, children who were never breastfed were forever stuck in the oral phase and destined to become either "Don Juans" or homosexuals because one either seeks the mother's love through other women or adopts the maternal into one's own identity. I always found that peculiar how well it applied to our own cases, but I suppose that's just anecdotal evidence.

My brother told me he never drank because while other people needed alcohol to overcome the fear of rejection and enjoy socializing, it was naturally fun for him. I thought that was a very intelligent thing to say. Eventually he told me he often wished he was still a child and asked if I ever felt the same way. I thought about it for a while and said that I had experienced something similar around the age of thirteen. I told him I thought it was a natural response to the fear of adulthood and the feeling of responsibility that that entails. Now I completely avoided anything that made me feel younger. Thinking about my childhood always instilled a sense of helplessness within me that I desperately wanted to avoid.

I thought back to my own first semester of college. I spent all my time in my dorm room playing League of Legends for twelve hours everyday. It probably sounds like an exaggeration, but it really wasn't. I was ashamed to think I wasted a year of my life playing a computer game I hated because I was so single mindedly obsessed with reaching diamond rank. As soon as I finally reached it during finals week, I never touched the game again - it was like I had finally been set free.

Still, I doubt I would have made any friends even if I hadn't played the game. I was too nervous and insecure for that. It's absurd really. If you worry about whether or not other people like you they don't, but if you truly don't give a shit they end up worrying about whether or not you like them.

The next weekend I received the call from Tom and Jeannie. They were concerned and wanted me to come back to their house for the weekend. I didn't want to. Being around them always made me feel like I was a child, but I didn't see anyway around that. It was arranged that they would pick me up from Iowa State so that we could have a long talk during the car ride back to their house.

When they arrived, they each gave me a hug because that is what parents are supposed to do when they see their child. I entered into Tom's SUV and sat in the passenger seat next to him. It was silent for a long while and I occupied myself by staring out of the window like I had done so much when I was younger. If I squinted my eyes just right I could make a game out of weaving a spec of dust on the window through the telephone poles.

Eventually Tom asked. "So what's going on?"

"Nothing," I replied. "I'm just bored of school and ready for something new."

Tom and Jeannie had a very hard time accepting that answer. They kept pressuring me to explain myself further, but I really couldn't - not to them anyway.

Jeannie started crying in the back seat.

"What will other people think?" She managed to choke out.

I found her to be completely disgusting. Presumably she was upset that she wouldn't be able to brag to her friends anymore that her son was a double major. I just wanted to get away from them.

"What's your plan?" Tom demanded to know.

I thought about it for a few minutes, but the question didn't really make sense to me. I just did what I felt like doing at any given moment.

Besides, how can one even plan when so much of life depends on external influences beyond your own control? I didn't plan on meeting Reanne, but knowing her had profoundly altered the course of my life, and I was really completely helpless to do anything about it. I thought about Kierkegaard's aphorism.

Life must be understood backwards without forgetting it must be lived forwards.

I couldn't quote Kierkegaard to Tom or he would think I was being pretentious.

Instead, I replied. "I would like to move to a big city and make my own money."

I could see Tom was fairly satisfied with that answer. He was a small business owner like his father and grandfather. I told him I couldn't stand the idea of working for anyone else, and I didn't like other people telling me what to do. Tom understood that. It was a very masculine thing to say after all.

There was no rationalizing with Jeannie. She was beyond hysterical at this point, but I couldn't really blame her. Sitting in the back seat always made me feel alone and left out of the conversation, so I could see how she might have felt like we weren't listening to her.

When we had finally arrived back in their neighborhood, I was overcome with such a shapeless feeling of dysphoria that it would be hard to describe. It was one of those new housing developments that had been built within the last ten years. It was after dark and the empty cul-de-sacs conveyed such an eerie sense of lifelessness as if the people who lived there would be doing the same unchanging daily routine until they dropped dead shopping for frozen pizzas at Wal Mart.

The place just seemed so open like there was no shelter from the elements and a strong wind could come at any minute and blow it all way. There were no trees, just saplings held upright in plastic tubes to keep them from collapsing underneath their own weight.

I looked up at the sky to see Orion, but I couldn't see anything but the belt because of the light pollution. I wanted to scream, but I stifled the impulse and went straight to my old bedroom. It felt just as lonely as I remembered it to be. It was a large house (far too large in my opinion) and filled with several useless spaces: a study without books, a guest room without guests, a game room without anyone to to play with, and even a Hawaiian themed sitting room despite the fact that no one in the household had ever taken a vacation to Hawaii.

I had a childhood friend growing up whose family was poor. Their house was small and falling apart, but I spent most of my time there. I liked how you could hear his mother making dinner in the kitchen and his father yelling at the TV during the Green Bay Packers game in the living room while we played videogames in my friend's bedroom which he shared with his older brother. It was so different from my own room in the basement where I wouldn't ever know if anyone else was even in the house. I had a lot of nightmares as a kid.

I wanted to smoke so I walked up the second staircase exiting through the garage. I didn't want to walk by Tom or Jeannie. They didn't know I smoked and I knew Jeannie would never let me hear the end of it if she found out.

It turned out I had anxiously smoked the last of my cigarettes while I was waiting for Tom and Jeannie to pick me up in Ames, so I borrowed my brother's car which he had left behind and went to the convenience store.

As I drove it occurred to me that the city was dieing. The primary employer, a cement plant, had closed down the year before. Everywhere I looked there were shops with broken windows that had been boarded up. The few people I saw looked tired and worn out. I couldn't make out what colors their clothes were, but they all looked gray to me.

Evidently the city council's promise to revitalize the downtown and attract new businesses to the area wasn't working which wasn't surprising considering their plan consisted of paving the area with colored bricks and installing sculptures (which were soon vandalized). The council wanted to turn the city into a "cultural center" and continuously reminded the citizens to be proud of their "musical heritage" on account of a native that had written a successful broadway musical sixty years ago. It didn't matter. Broadway was a long ways away and the city was exclusively known as a place to buy cheap methamphetamine by outsiders.

I arrived at the convenience store and was acknowledged by a rather frumpy looking woman with a wart on her chin. I asked her for a pack of Marlboro Black (the cigarettes with the most fashionable packaging) and handed her my ID.

"This doesn't look like you." She said gloatingly after she had taken a quick look.

I was surprised. No one had ever refused my ID before. I assured her that it was, in fact, me in the picture, but she refused to sell me the cigarettes and asked me to leave.

On the way back to my car I took a look at my ID and I had to admit to myself that the frumpy woman was right - it didn't look like me at all.

The picture was a little more than three years old, and I had a buzzcut, wore a tie, and smiled. The picture disgusted me. I would never wear a tie anymore (it looked try-hard. Fashion has to come off as nonchalant even if you take special care to put a fashionable black pen in your shirt pocket.) and I certainly wouldn't smile anymore. I read a study that showed how smiling is the least attractive facial expression to women. It makes you look weak. I felt embarrassed that I had been unintentionally showing this photo to people every time I bought cigarettes.

I returned to Tom and Jeannie's house empty handed My head was pounding. I wanted a cigarette in the worst way, but I didn't want to go to another gas station and show another person the embarrassing photo on my ID.

Walking through the house to get back to my room I passed by a mirror and noticed a blemish situated on my left cheek. I stopped dead in my tracks and stared at my reflection, but I didn't see my reflection. All I saw was the blemish. It seemed to grow larger every second. I was unable to look away. I stood there for several hours paralyzed by the fact that it was there on my cheek and there was nothing I could do to immediately get rid of it. It occurred to me how ugly I was, and I began to cry. I went to bed and wrapped myself in the sheets like a cocoon just as I had done to sooth myself when I was a child. I reassured myself that my perception was off; I was just in nicotine withdrawal but I was unable to calm myself down. I wished I was back at school where I could go to the library and be admired. There was no one. I was just lying there alone in my room.

The next day I occupied myself with Tom and Jeannie's desktop computer. I spent several hours reading articles on Wikipedia, but none of them were useful or had any redeeming scholarly merit. I wondered about how people lived before the Internet. It must have been terrible living with all of that uncertainty. I can't imagine seeing a bottle of ketchup and not being able to immediately read all about the history of the condiment. Did you know that it started out as a Chinese sauce made out of pickled fish?

I started to wonder what Michael was up to. Michael lived two doors down and was a close friend of mine, probably the only one I really had to confide into. We had a lot in common though people wouldn't have guessed. Michael was two years younger than myself and had become something of a social pariah as of late for dropping out of high school. It annoyed me that everyone presumed to judge him as lazy and unmotivated when they had no idea what it was actually like to be him.

Michael was also adopted though he was actually the child of a rape - I never envied him for that. I had enough trouble accepting the circumstances of my own birth and it was entirely consensual. The guy was troubled. There's no doubt about that, but he always seemed to completely understand me when I talked, and when he talked I always had to admit that I usually thought and felt the same way he did.

I sent him a text message asking him if he wanted to hang out.

He immediately responded. *sure*

I drove over to his house and waited twenty-two minutes before he came out. When I saw him, I could tell that something wasn't quite right with him the way he shuffled when he walked. I asked if he wanted to get something to eat. He mumbled a few words of agreement so I drove to McDonalds and we sat across from each other. It was slightly passed midnight and we were the only ones there.

I looked at Michael across the table. He was a very attractive guy, androgynous in appearance the same way I was. He had beautifully arched jet black eyebrows which stood in stark contrast to his brown, curly hair, and while his full lips always bore a subtle expression of cruelty, you never really noticed it because his bright bluish-green eyes seemed to sparkle in a way that captured your full attention. Like me, he was keenly aware of how he could enhance his appearance by wearing black. I loved being around him. He was so beautiful I felt that it added to my own appearance just to be seen with him.

He was different from the last time I saw him. His eyes were half closed and he showed no emotion in his face whatsoever. It was difficult to get him to talk and when he did he sounded extremely paranoid (something about how the dealer he was buying from was lacing the marijuana with PCP in order to destroy his customer's minds so that he could be the only functioning human in a world of zombies).

I was getting worried. I continued to ask him questions.

So what's new with you? Watch any good shows on Netflix? Fucked any girls?

All of a sudden his eyes opened wide up and in an instant he appeared and acted normally again. We then proceeded to have a lively conversation about everything that was going on in our lives. I learned that he hadn't left his basement in several weeks and hadn't had anything to do but play League of Legends. I thought that explained why he had been acting so odd. I knew from personal experience that social isolation did really bizarre things to the human mind.

We talked about how manipulative you had to be to keep girls from leaving you. It was refreshing; most people would look at me like I was a terrible person if I told them I intentionally made a girl cry to keep her emotionally invested, but not Michael. He actually understood the way the world really is. On that same note, he was one of the few people who could engage me on purely abstract topics. It upset me that other people thought he was stupid when he was more politically and philosophically aware than the lot of them.

He had great stories especially about drugs. He had tried everything from the common psychedelics to obscure opioids and dissociatives I hadn't even heard of. I asked him about rehab. I had heard he had been forced to go after a string of arrests for possession of paraphernalia. The question immediately launched him into an angry tirade.

"It's all a scam, dude." he said with total conviction. "And the psychiatrists they employ are talentless hacks. All they do is open up the DSM-V and tell you what you already know. I could do that myself."

I laughed. That was exactly the impression I had always had of them.

"They're easy to fool though." He added. "If you fake ADD you can get a prescription for Adderall and make a shitload of money selling it."

It impressed me how clever he must be to actually execute a scheme like that.

When we had finished eating, we decided to take a drive. It's a rather enjoyable pastime really. There are hardly any other cars on Iowa county highways so you can go as fast as you want. Throw loud music into the mix and it really starts to get fun.

Michael asked me if I had ever had a bad trip. I replied that I had. I thought back to it. It was almost exactly one year ago. At the time it had occurred to me that I was a rather boring person, so I wanted to do everything I could to make myself more interesting for Reanne.

I bought a tab of LSD from my roommate (a rather mysterious fellow, we lived together for a year and only had two conversations, both when we were pretty fucked up) and tucked it into my lower lip at precisely 10:00 A.M on a Saturday morning. I was so excited with the prospect of trying something new my heart was pounding and I was sweating profusely. Thirty minutes later I was overcome with an extreme feeling of nausea as the drug began to take effect and objects began to reflect a small tint of translucent purple light. I rushed to the bathroom and vomited for several minutes. The toilet was alive and sucking out my soul. I felt an overwhelming sense of dread for what I had gotten myself into. I felt trapped within my dorm room, and I needed to escape so I resolved to walk over to the forest. It was a perfect 72°F autumn day, and as I stepped outside

I was bombarded with sensory stimulation. I could see everything in my field of vision simultaneously and all the sounds were individually distinguishable.

When I arrived at the forest, I became an adventurer exploring new terrain. The trees were a thick rainforest and the narrow paths that ran along the deep ravines led to Mordor. After an entire lifetime of exploring I looked off the ledge at a tall hill in the distance. There were two colors. The Green Life was doing battle with the Brown Death and the Brown Death was winning, easily. I looked down into the ravine and noticed it was filled with hundreds of disfigured corpses and crawling with spiders. My attention was drawn to a decaying plant which dripped with decay and audibly exhaled Death onto its surroundings. I hightailed it back to my dorm room because it was getting dark, and I didn't even want to know what sort of Demons would come out at night. I looked in the mirror and what I saw was truly horrifying - the skin was melting off of my face. I saw my own skull, and what made it worse, I saw the expression of pure unadulterated terror on my own face as it happened.

I was so shaken up by the experience I didn't have a single conversation with another person for about six months. I was unable to function socially even if I would have wanted to - the inner anxiety and discomfort I felt occupied my full attention. Maybe if Reanne wasn't in Greece I could have embraced her and had a good cry to get it out of my system, but I kind of doubt she would have been comfortable with that. I guess I'll never know.

I recounted my experience to Michael and he understood. It was refreshing to be with somebody who understood. I listened to his story too.

"Christopher," he paused. "If I had access to a gun, there is no way I wouldn't have killed myself. There was nothing but pain." We stayed silent after that.

I thought about World War II. A whole generation of boys fought and saw horrible things. Many of the survivors experienced severe post traumatic stress and were unable to ever recover. Those that did became tougher than they ever could have been otherwise. Was it worth it then, to suffer so much if it made you grow as a person? Michael and I were the survivors, and what difference did it make to us whether the horrors we saw were real or just in our own minds? They were real to us and we were stronger for having experienced them.

By the time we returned to our Cul-de-Sac we were completely out of topics to discuss. Michael offered me a cigarette which was a relief (I had been hoping he would), and we stood together in silence in the middle of the street. It felt nice to smoke with somebody else for a change.

When we had finished, I turned to Michael and said "Take care of yourself, man." with complete sincerity in my tone. Michael looked at me for a moment as if he was confused because he didn't know how to respond to the genuine nature of my comment, but his face softened and he responded "You too, dude." in the same fashion.

The next morning I awoke earlier than usual at about 10:00 A.M., eager to return to my own apartment. I contacted a friend, Luke, from high school who visited his parents every weekend to secure a ride back to Ames. He would be by at 11:30 to pick me up. I walked upstairs to where Tom and Jeannie were making breakfast and entertained myself by reading the local newspaper. It's humorous, the types of stories they have to print to fill a local newspaper. The front page was devoted to a local man who collected egg-related memorabilia.

Jeannie fried three eggs and ham and placed it in front of me without speaking. Tom walked over to the table and, standing across from me, began to implore me to stay in school. It was a futile gesture. The more they told me to stay in school the more I wanted to leave. Jeannie started crying again, and while I was annoyed, I couldn't really be upset with them. They talked as if I would be homeless without a college degree. I suppose it was different for them when they were my age. They were both Boomers born in the late fifties and had both done well for themselves after attending college, but it just wasn't like that anymore. I read that 50% of today's college graduates are still living with their parents at the age of twenty-five. I shuddered to think about it. I would rather put a bullet in my head if it came to that.

When I couldn't take it anymore, I walked back downstairs into the basement without saying anything and waited for my ride alone. At precisely 11:30 the doorbell rang and I collected my things and made my way to the door. On the way out, Tom and Jeannie each gave me a hug because that is what parents are supposed to do when their child leaves, and Tom slipped forty dollars into my hand and whispered "Here's some cash. Don't tell your mother and don't spend it on cigarettes." I thanked him, but couldn't help but to smile knowing full well that I would. I think he knew it as well, but the way he patted me on the back gave me the impression that despite what he actually said about staying in school he was prouder than he had ever been.

I handed Luke my bag, and he put it in the trunk of his precious Cadillac while I took my place in the backseat and admired the perfectly maintained leather interior. Jason, Luke's roommate and another friend from high school, was seated slouched in the passenger seat. We greeted each other with "What's up?" but it was just a formality and a conversation didn't materialize.

Luke turned on the engine and the car was filled with the familiar sound of Billy Joel. Luke's Cadillac contained all twelve albums, and it was all he ever listened to. Whenever River of Dreams finished playing Luke immediately and without hesitation pressed "1" to start back over again at Cold Spring Harbor. Today we had the pleasure of listening to Turnstiles.

"Christ," I said, "I swear to God you're a Boomer trapped inside a Millennial's body."

"You're damn right I am." Luke replied.

It was true. Luke worked at the municipal golf course and had picked up all of their mannerisms. It was actually pretty annoying how he always bragged about drinking his coffee black.

We didn't talk at all during the car ride which most people might find uncomfortable, but we just accepted it as normal. We spent a lot of time together in high school, but had since grown pretty far apart.

While Luke was sociable, I was embarrassed to be seen with him in public. He wore nothing but T-shirts with gym shorts and still sported the same buzzcut he had in Kindergarten. He played it off like he was proud of the way he looked, like he wasn't vain like the rest of us, but I always got the impression he was simply afraid of trying something new. Despite hanging out exclusively with stoners, he never tried the stuff himself and claimed he never would. He wouldn't drink alcohol or smoke cigarettes either. He was completely straight edge. How someone could be satisfied watching Seinfeld every weekend was beyond me, but he didn't really seem all that satisfied I had to admit. Nor did he seem unsatisfied - he was just sort of blank.

Jason, by contrast, was very fashionable, but he suffered from a crippling social anxiety that made it truly embarrassing to introduce him to anyone. I pitied him. Every now and then he would confide in me that he was bored with life and that he wished he could make a friend, but he never made any effort to join a club or even speak to anyone else in class. I would invite him to come lift with me and he would for a session or two before he would send me a text *I don't feel like going today* and skip out to smoke marijuana and watch anime.

Occasionally, I felt a twinge of sadness because we weren't as close as we used to be, but I guess we weren't all that close to begin with. We just sat together at lunch and told each other jokes we'd read on 4chan because there was no one else at our small Catholic school who shared our sense of humor, and now that I think about it, I think we were all secretly harboring antisocial attitudes towards each other. It was like that movie The Comedy with Tim Heidecker where they all hang out and make sarcastic comments like "Boy, I sure do love hanging out with all of my great friends."

I focused on the Billy Joel that was currently playing in Luke's Cadillac. Despite the fact that I always ripped on Luke for listening to Dad Rock, I secretly loved Billy Joel. The song Captain Jack perfectly captured the disinterest my peers seemed to have in the world, and it seemed utterly ahead of its time considering it was written forty years ago. I suppose that's the thing about good art - it's so representative of the human condition so as to become timeless.

James was playing now, and it was obvious that Billy was speaking directly to me.

Are you still in school? Living up to expectations?

I started to tear up without making any noise, thank God. The last thing I would want is for Luke or Jason to see me like that.

When will you write your masterpiece?

The tears intensified. I had started many projects before, but I always gave up shortly after starting. How could you focus long enough to create something in an age where you always have the option of watching youtube videos or playing mobile games on your smartphone? Besides, even if you did manage to write something, who would even take the time to read it when any reader constantly lives with the same distractions?

Immediately after James was Prelude/Angry Young Man, one of my favorites both musically and lyrically. I thought back to last semester when Reanne was in Greece and I was recovering from my trip. I was angry all day long, every day, from the moment I got up in the morning to the moment I finally fell asleep at night. I don't just mean angry either. I mean a ceaselessly wrathful, petulant rage directed inward at myself because how unreasonable is it to be that angry over trivial things? Someone would accidentally bump into me in the cafeteria, and I would be bedridden for days.

Miami 2017 was playing while Luke dropped me off at my apartment. I decided I would move to Miami after the semester was over, but I would need to come up with a better reason than *I heard it in a Billy Joel song.*

"We should go get dinner sometime." Luke said as I was stepping out of his Cadillac.

"That would be fun." I replied knowing full well it wasn't going to happen. I think he knew it too. I looked over at Jason, but he kept his headphones on and didn't react.

It was about dinner time, and as I was starving for attention I decided to eat at the school's dining center. I rarely did because it was so expensive ($11) but every now and then it was nice not to have to cook for myself. I took my copy of *The Picture of Dorian Gray* from my bedroom and began to walk over to the dining center. I had already read the book through several times, but I thought it was definitely a fashionable book to be seen reading.

I stopped by the convenience store on my way to buy another pack of cigarettes and felt extremely self-conscious about my outdated photo when I handed the clerk my ID. He sold me the pack without looking at it. I thought back to the homely woman who had refused it and figured she had just been bored and needed some sort of commotion to bring color to her day. She might have even enjoyed the feeling of power. I didn't really blame her. After all life must be terribly harsh if you're homely. Jean Paul Sartre himself said all his philosophy was an attempt to come to grips with his own ugliness.

It really is unfair how people shape their opinion of you based entirely off of how you look. If you have a high opinion of yourself and you're ugly you're arrogant. If you have a high opinion of yourself and you're beautiful you're confident. If you keep to yourself and you're ugly, you're creepy. If you keep to yourself and you're beautiful, you're mysterious. I could go on and on with examples, but I think an exceedingly intelligent person like yourself, my dear reader, gets the idea. I even read that physically attractive people make 10% more money at their jobs. It's profoundly unfair, but I just thank God that I got the better end of the deal.

There was a guy who lived in my dorm freshman year, utterly hideous in appearance. The things everyone said about him were horrible, and he never did anything to deserve such treatment. In fact, it was obvious the kid just wanted to make some friends. I wish I could tell you that I did the noble thing and befriended him myself, but I couldn't. I found him repulsive. That's the limitation with introspection. I could understand myself perfectly, but still be unable to change myself for the better. At least everyone else had the ability to externalize their disgust onto him. I had to internalize it and feel like I was an utterly shallow person.

I saw Cody walking towards me on the sidewalk. He was also somebody that I knew from my time living in the dorms. He would stop and talk to me; he was one of those people who stops and talks to everyone he comes into contact with and remains painfully unaware whether or not the other person is enjoying the conversation. I had no way of avoiding him.

When we were within speaking range, he immediately began telling me all about this great new computer game he bought and the exciting (in his words) legislation he was bringing forward to the student government. I rolled my eyes internally as I imagined it - a room filled with 300 college students utterly convinced of their self-importance arguing endlessly about what color the school's recycling bins should be. Bored as I was, I didn't dare leave the conversation too soon. The last thing I needed was for everyone to hear about how rude I was.

"So where are you headed?" he asked.

"Conversations" I said. That was the trendy name for the dining center.

"Did you walk all the way from your apartment?" he asked, incredulously.

"Yes."

"Well, why didn't you take the bus?" he asked with an equivalent display of puzzletude.

"I guess I just prefer walking." I answered, truthfully.

Cody looked at me like I was crazy and paused before he said "Listen man, I've got to get to an executive board meeting for the biology club."

"Good talking to you." I said, laughing to myself. Now instead of hearing about how rude I was, people would hear about how strange I was for walking everywhere. That's how it goes I suppose. Some people were born to be talked about.

There's that famous quote. I forgot who said it. *Great minds discuss ideas, good minds discuss events, and small minds discuss people.* There were a lot of small minds at Iowa State University. The few times I hung around the other people who lived in the dorms all they ever did was gossip about whichever one of their friends was currently absent. I hated them all, but I couldn't help but to wonder what they said about me when I wasn't there.

I entered the dining center which was located on the bottom floor of the girls only dorm (which made it the best place to eat) and I told the cute girl who was usually at the register swiping student ID cards "I like what you did with your hair." She had just died it red. She blushed and looked away as I made a mental note to completely ignore her the next time I saw her.

I piled my plate with steak and french fries (it was Friday) and took a seat by myself at the corner table. On one side of me there was a group of Black students all dressed in sweatsuits and on the other was a group of Asian students who were all dressed rather well - black shirts and skinny jeans. The rest of the cafeteria was made up of whites who appeared to be grouped by style on first glance, but they were actually divided up by majors. Ag students wore thick plaid flannels with baggy jeans and cowboy boots. Business types always wore oxfords and slacks. Engineers never had any fashion sense at all (graphic tees and sneakers - Yuck!), and of course there were plenty of sorority girls in their God awful yogas.

It's funny really, if you think about how every college pamphlet shows a black, white, asian, and handicapped kid all sitting together and laughing. In reality nothing like that would ever happen. Like everything else it goes back to evolutionary psychology. *Only associate with people who look and think like you do. They're the only ones you can trust.* Racism is instinctual just like everything else that's wrong with the human condition, especially the sadistic impulse and that's what makes it terrifying.Our ancestors who saw someone they didn't recognize going after the same gazelle and stuck a pointy stick in the strange looking person's stomach survived. The people who went over to share had a pointy stick thrust in their own stomach. Violence isn't senseless at all. It makes perfect sense if you think about it.

As I ate, I opened The Picture of Dorian Gray to a little passed the halfway point and pretended to scan the pages with my eyes. I noticed a girl I sort of knew looking at me from a few tables away. I think her name was Molly or maybe Megan? She was one of those ambitious career-type girls. I think she was the Treasurer for her sorority or something. I critiqued her paper in a class once.

She was wearing a tight brown skirt that went down to her mid-thigh and a white blouse. I started to lust after her, and I wanted to go and talk to her, but it would look desperate if I approached her - like she wouldn't have to work for my attention so I decided against it.

When I finished my meal, I walked over to the cashier and took a toothpick from the holder hoping to make eye contact with the cute girl who swiped my card, but a large group of students had just walked in and she was busy dealing with them. I was disappointed, but then I began to wonder whether or not she was ignoring me on purpose.

That bitch, I thought. *I wasn't even really that attracted to her in the first place.*

I exited the dining center and was lighting a cigarette when I felt a tap on my shoulder.

"Living dangerously are we?"

I turned around and found myself face to face with Reanne who was grinning wildly. Behind her was another wimpy looking guy, a different one from the last time I saw her. I stared into her eyes and felt a jolt of pleasure course through me like electricity. I knew she felt it too. We just stood there looking into each other's eyes for what seemed like several minutes without saying a single word.

Eventually, I broke the silence. "It's good to see you, Reanne."

"It's good to see you too, Christopher." she replied.

I turned my back on her and walked back to my apartment, snapping my fingers every time I stepped over a crack in the sidewalk.

When I had returned to my apartment, I tried to entertain myself by continuing to read Byron's Don Juan, but I was having trouble focusing. I kept thinking about Reanne and how delightfully erratic her behavior was.

Late at night around 1:00 my phone buzzed and when I checked my messages I saw that I had received a text from Reanne.

Christopher I miss you.

I immediately responded with the truth. *I miss you too Reanne. I hope you know I have a lot of respect for you, I just don't trust you at all.*

Reanne responded immediately. *Haha that's okay, I probably wouldn't trust me either. You're so fascinating to me though, I keep wondering how you spend all of your time.*

I replied. *Well I read mostly, have you ever heard of How to Win Friends and Influence People or 48 Laws of Power? I feel like an ambitious person like yourself could really find those books useful.*

Reanne responded. *Haha we are ambitious people aren't we? I'll make sure to check them out! Remember when you told me everything we could accomplish together?*

I smiled to myself. After a year and a half of careful planning and social maneuvering I finally had her in the palm of my hand. I thought back to everything I had done. Using drugs to become more interesting, publically faking a religious conversion so she would think we were soulmates, the lifting, cunning use of social media with every post and picture with the sole purpose of attracting her attention, it all led up to this moment right now, where I could finally have the pleasure of my revenge. I composed the text message to end all text messages, and into it I poured all of my cruelty.

Listen Reanne, I want you to know the truth. The truth is I will never marry you. I will fuck you whenever you want me to, but I will NEVER marry you. I loved you once, but I will never allow myself to ever feel that way again. The way you had the audacity to insinuate that you could ever find someone better than me is something I could never forgive. Your sheer ignorance revealed by the fact that you would ever entertain the notion that somebody better than me could possibly exist is utterly unforgivable. It would do you well to stop thinking of me as a backup plan to achieving your own status in life. The truth is you need me a hell of a lot more than I would ever need you.

Reanne sent back a rather long and rambling message that I won't bother including in this text. It was all about how sorry she was for what had happened in Greece. It reeked of insecurity, and to tell you the truth it seemed so weak I couldn't understand what I had ever seen in her in the first place. I didn't respond after that. I was finally bored with her. I went back to reading. I could actually focus now.

Part 3

The next few weeks went differently for me. I no longer felt the need to wander aimlessly around campus. I had always thought that I had the ability to work on some interesting project if only I could free myself from the infinite distraction of my emotional life. After several years, probably not since Jessica dumped me at the end of the 8th grade I finally felt at peace enough to really focus. I couldn't think of any specific reason for the change in my thinking.

I spent most of my time at the library and checked out many of the books I never had a chance to read: Augustine's Confessions, The Old Man and the Sea, and American Psycho to name a few. Occasionally I would think of Reanne, but I tried to text her once and discovered she had blocked me again so she was quickly fading from my mind. Besides, there were plenty of other girls to be seen at the library.

It's funny, there's a whole building with shelves upon shelves of books but all I ever saw was people with laptops checking Facebook. One time while I was reading a petite girl with dark skin, dark eyes, and dark hair came over to me and asked what I was doing. She had such exquisitely delicate and feminine facial features and I was so overcome with desire that I had to ignore her and find another place to sit. It was annoying, but some things never change I suppose.

I checked my email. My inbox was filled with messages from TA's who informed that I failed their class. To think that receiving a message like that a year ago would have sent me into a panic amused me to no end. It meant absolutely nothing to me now. The message from my speech communications TA was the longest. It went on and on about how there was absolutely zero chance to turn my grade around since I had violated the attendance requirements spelled out in his syllabus. The tone of the email conveyed a sense of pleasure like he enjoyed the power he wielded to issue grades and hoped I would respond pleading for a second chance. His email was the only one I replied to.

Thanks for informing me. Have a good one. Was all I sent. I figured that would piss him off and it brought me great pleasure to imagine him opening it up and closing it in a huff, his face bright red.

Late at night, I was returning to my apartment and smoking when I passed by a rather young looking mother who was pulling her son (about five years old I presume) along by the hand. She glared at me as I passed and let out a forced cough as if to scold me for polluting her son's air.

Christ, I thought, *what a cunt. As if they even had a trace of second hand smoke considering how windy it is.*

Nevertheless, I didn't feel like smoking anymore and I threw my cigarette away though it was only half smoked. I couldn't stop thinking about the mother and how she had instinctively reacted to protect her son from even the most imaginary threat. It made me think of my own mother, or rather the idea I had of her. Truthfully I didn't know a single thing about her, but she seemed as real to me as anybody else.

Why wasn't I good enough for her? I thought as my eyes began to water. I was still about five minutes walking distance from my apartment and it took all of my strength to keep from breaking down into childish sobs. It made me angry to think about all of the encouragement she likely received.

"It's so selfless what you're doing, sweetie. You're giving him a better life."

Was it a better life? The fact that I was all alone and pushed everyone away from me? The fact I couldn't trust anyone? It was all that whore's fault. I bet she was screwing some other man the day after she gave me away. I shoved my face into my pillow and sobbed uncontrollably for twenty minutes. When the sadness had passed, I felt surprisingly good and full of energy. I had to admit that as pathetic as it was to cry, I always felt much better afterwards.

I was overcome with a strong sense of ambition. I had to make something of myself. I had to become somebody powerful and important with lots of money. Then I would find my mother and watch her cry. I fell asleep easily that night feeling very satisfied with myself.

The next day I awoke much earlier than normal at about 9:00 AM. and after frying up three eggs and ham I returned to the library determined to educate myself thoroughly on some useful skill with which to make my fortune. I considered computer programming, but I quickly decided against it.

That's what all the millennials think will make them rich. They want to make some brand new social networking app that will "revolutionize the way we all communicate."

That made me sick. Social media was just a way for people to brag to each other about how perfect their lives were even when they weren't having face to face conversations. I wanted no part in that. Instead, I decided to study real estate. Why exactly it popped into my head I couldn't tell you, but it seemed like something none of my peers were thinking about so it surely had potential.

I checked out nearly every book I could find on property valuation and mortgages as well as one particular book that caught my eye as I was looking for the others. It was an old book from the early 1960's. It was a psychological book of case studies on the personalities of self-made men. I read through it first. It was interesting. Instead of portraying the men as heroes, as noble captains of industry, it portrayed them as troubled men motivated by a pathological need to control everything as a result of deeply ingrained insecurities. I found the book altogether reassuring. I had a lot in common with the men in the case studies.

Luckily, I was able to sit in my spot at the top of the stairs. Comfortable, I proceeded to pour through the stack of books and absorb their technical information. It's funny really, how hard it is to read four pages of a textbook when it's assigned to you, but how easy it is to read four hundred pages of a book you check out yourself.

By mid afternoon I was ready to take a break so I walked over to the coffeeshop for a sandwich and cappuccino. I noticed an acquaintance of mine, Andrew, sitting alone at a table looking at his phone so I decided to sit with him. We were fairly good friends back when I lived in the dorm, and I hadn't seen him in a while. He had spent the previous semester in Edinburgh.

After a little bit of the usual small talk, he felt comfortable enough with me to tell me about his life abroad. He hadn't enjoyed it at all. He found himself alone often and left out from all of the other groups of students who seemed to already have known each other.

Poor guy, I thought. *He had probably anticipated that a semester abroad would be filled with constant traveling and meeting new people.*

He was an average looking guy, a little overweight, but nothing too hideous. Still, he didn't stand out and when you don't stand out your life is going to be boring whether you are at Iowa State, Edinburgh, or anywhere for that matter.

He began telling me about a girl he had been seeing and developed rather strong feelings for. He told me he wanted to take things to the next level and was going to ask her to be his girlfriend. I started laughing at him.

Didn't he realize how moronic that was? As if simply calling their relationship boyfriend/girlfriend would change anything about it.

I tried to tell him he needed her to see him with other girls so she would get jealous, and he needed to fuck her because female orgasms release oxytocin which would make her fall in love with him but he wouldn't listen to my advice. In fact, he just looked at me like I was some sort of monster. I watched him compose and send the text message in front of me, presumably just because I told him not to.

Five minutes later he received a message in response.

I would love to be your girlfriend. :)

Andrew showed me the message and looked rather pleased with himself for having, in his mind, proved me wrong. I managed to let out a polite "I hope it works out for you." through my building hostility as I excused myself from his presence and started heading back to the library.

For a split second I considered that I might be wrong about Romance. I happened to know the girl he was involved with, a rather average looking person herself. Maybe they were mutually in love and the secret to a successful relationship was simply to be average looking? I thought that was not likely upon further consideration. I had asked Andrew if she had ever texted him first. He replied that she didn't, but that was just the way she was - she didn't like texting. I doubted it. She probably just liked his attention, and was committed to doing whatever happened to be necessary in order to maintain it. I had half a mind to pursue her myself and show Andrew everytime she texted me first, but I decided that would be mean-spirited and had no intention of expending that much effort just to make a point.

I returned to the library to continue my reading, but was unable to procure my usual spot. In fact, there was no place at all to sit in the main area. It annoyed me. There must have been an organic chemistry test coming up or something because everywhere I looked there were groups of students huddled around each other and holding flashcards. Amusing really how much effort they were putting in to memorize molecular diagrams that would be quickly forgotten the day after the test. I admit I was slightly envious. It seemed like such a good way to flirt with girls.

I had to go all the way to the fourth floor before I could find a place to sit and even then it was a small wooden desk practically pushed up against a bookcase. I tried to continue reading as diligently as I had before, but I was distracted by the rings in the wood. They interlocked to form an uncanny image of a naked woman complete with breasts and a vagina. I thought it was hilarious and eagerly looked around for someone to show it to, but everyone around me had their headphones in and I didn't know any of them anyway. I traced out the image with my pen and satisfied myself with the knowledge that the next person who sat there would see it.

I opened up the book I was reading, but everytime I tried to read the words I didn't understand what I had read. It was like I heard the words in my mind but didn't understand what they meant. After reading the same paragraph four or five times in a row to no avail I decided to call it quits. I kept thinking about Andrew's contention that all you have to do is be honest with a girl. It seemed silly to me, but I thought I might as well try it out for myself. I composed Reanne an email (I looked up her address on the Iowa State online directory) telling her that while I knew we both liked to play games, I admired her and wanted to spend time with her. After I sent the email, I compulsively checked my inbox every ten minutes until I finally gave up on the idea of receiving a response four days later. It annoyed me that I had no way of knowing whether she hadn't read my email, had read it and ignored it out of spite, or had been so confused by an action so out of character she didn't know how to respond.

When it was the weekend before Thanksgiving break, I was faced with the decision of whether or not to return to Tom and Jeannie's house or spend an entire week alone on a deserted campus. It was a tough choice between two unpleasant options. On one hand I dreaded having to listen to Tom and Jeannie nag me about my future, but on the other I didn't really want to spend an entire weekend alone in my apartment either. There was no point in going to the library if there was nobody there to admire me. The decision was made for me, however, when my brother called and asked if I would pick him up at the University of Northern Iowa. I agreed since I didn't have anything better to do.

It had started snowing as soon as I left Ames, and by the time I reached my brother's dorm it was really coming down hard. I called my brother to let him know that I had arrived. I hadn't seen him in several months but he looked exactly the same. He was extremely small at around five foot five and 105 pounds which caused a rather comical effect when paired with his extremely deep voice. He wasn't ugly, but he had an enormous hooked nose which attracted your full attention. He dressed in the preppy brand clothes like American Eagle or Abercrombie that had the brand written across the front in big letters. While I usually couldn't stand those sorts of clothes (to be a walking billboard is to spit in the face of originality, the only thing that is really fashionable), I actually thought he was able to pull it off rather well.

"Mom called. She wants us to stay here tonight. Apparently there's supposed to be a full on blizzard."

Knowing Jeannie didn't want me to drive back to their house made me absolutely convinced that I would.

"Doesn't matter." I said. "We're going."

"Are you sure?" My brother asked. "I've seen the way you drive."

There he goes again, I thought, *knowing exactly how to push my buttons.*

"Yes, I'm sure." I said, my tone quite a bit more hostile than I intended.

I pulled onto the interstate and immediately regretted my decision. Since the road was so icy, I could only drive about thirty miles per hour which irritated me since I preferred to go much faster. There were cars in the ditch everywhere. Directly in front of me was a bright yellow pickup truck.

Perfect, I thought, *I'll just follow this guy the whole way.*

As soon as I had finished the thought, the yellow pickup truck spun out of control and ended up in the ditch. That was when the danger of the situation struck me and I felt a rush of adrenaline. My hands clenched the steering wheel tightly, and my eyes opened up wide - I was having fun.

My brother started talking. It was just the usual chit-chat and I don't remember much. We talked for a long time since the trip was taking about three times longer than it would without a snowstorm. Eventually my brother asked a rather thought provoking question.

"Don't you just find other people fascinating? Like you see them and you wonder what their life story is?"

I thought about it for a moment before I replied. "No. I really don't ever think about anyone but myself."

I could tell he believed me, but he wasn't judgemental about it either which I appreciated.

I turned off of the interstate at the exit before the one I should have taken. My brother had the GPS going on his phone and I instinctively took its directions without thinking. It turned out to be quite a big mistake because the route led us through twelve miles of uncleared back county highways.

Having had no problems so far, my mind began to wander and I was wondering how Keanne was spending her Thanksgiving break when my car hit an icy spot that sent my car spinning into the ditch.

"I knew we should have listened to Jeannie," my brother said rather self-righteously. "You could have gotten me killed."

As usual I ignored him. He was being overdramatic, and I had no intention of being sucked into his emotional games. I was just beginning to consider how to proceed since my car was stuck and I was unable to drive myself out of the ditch when a pickup truck stopped and offered to pull us out. I laughed to myself because of the sheer improbability and convenience of the situation.

It reminded me of the previous summer when I had been driving to my brother's high school graduation. I was thinking to myself about how there would never be any negative consequences for my actions since I was so good looking when my car ran out of gas in the middle of an intersection. I knew the tank had been low on fuel, but I simply hadn't bothered to take the time to fill it up. A tow truck immediately stopped and a man got out.

"What's the problem here?" He asked.

"Nothing serious." I said. "I'm just out of gas."

He replied that he had some and brought over a red plastic jug. After he filled up my car, I offered to give him twenty dollars, but he smiled, refused, and wished me a good day.

After I resumed driving, I was struck by such a feeling of anxiety such that I could not even fully appreciate the cosmic irony of having one of my theories so undisputedly proved only seconds after I had thought it up.

Through the most astounding irresponsibility, I had put myself in such an inconvenient situation only to be immediately spared any unpleasantness of my own doing.

My anxiety stemmed from the fact that my thoughts before the situation occurred so closely predicted the events that followed. It was much more than a simple coincidence. It was a premonition, but I was unable to decipher its exact meaning. An act of divine providence perhaps? A chance to reflect and consider the nature of my own character? Perhaps it was a rare insight into the solipsistic nature of the Universe? Maybe I'm actually the only person who really exists? It seems rather unfair, to exist and not be me. Maybe my thoughts had the power to affect the fabric of reality itself? I didn't know, and that is precisely what irritated me.

I watched the man tie a cable to the front of my car. He was tall, bearded, and wearing one of those tan workman's coats over a red flannel shirt. He looked like the quintessential country-living blue collar everyman.

"You guys sure are lucky that I happened to come along." He said as he worked. "Otherwise it would have been quite the sticky situation."

He laughed, but I didn't. I was too enraged by the condescension implied by his statement, but as much as I hated it, I did need his help so I gritted my teeth and kept my composure.

After he pulled my car from the ditch, he wished my brother and I well and instructed me to drive safely like I was a stupid child. I resumed driving, but my mind was occupied with thoughts about the man. I could see him all smug and self-righteous about having done the morally superior thing by stopping and helping. It annoyed me that he was unaware his actions were motivated by the pursuit of that feel good sensation he was currently feeling, the "Helper's High" they call it. It never occurred to him that his prosocial behavior was nothing more than an accident of brain chemistry, and he was just a few alleles off from driving by callously as I would have done had the situation been reversed. The exact gene is the one that codes for monoamine oxidase A. There's a particular variant that causes a deficiency of serotonin levels in the brain which produces dark, brooding, moods and antisocial behavior.

I remember one time I was playing at Friday Night Magic with Fabian when he dropped his box of dice causing them to scatter all over the floor. Everyone else immediately bent down to help Fabian pick up the dice, like they were acting instinctively without thought. I was the only person still standing in the room. I felt defective. I felt exposed.

I continued to drive, and I was struck by that same bout of anxiety I had experienced after the time I had run out of gas.

That's it. I thought. *The Universe is undoubtedly solipsistic. Everything and everyone exists solely for the purpose of creating the singular life-experience of me.*

I began to light a cigarette. My brother objected.

"You are not giving me cancer." He said indignantly.

I ignored him and continued on. He began screaming and gasping for air as he hastened to roll down the window while the blizzard raged on.

What a baby. I thought and threw the cigarette out my window.

"Just don't tell Jeannie about this." I commanded. I couldn't bear her *I told you so* attitude. My brother looked down.

When we had arrived at Tom and Jeannie's house, Jeannie rushed to my brother and I and threw her arms around us.

"There's my boys! I've been worried sick about you!" She exclaimed with the same inflection as somebody playing the role of a mother on a television show. I didn't return the hug. I was too disgusted for that.

"I was scared Mom. You should have seen the way Christopher was driving. He even smoked and now I have a sore throat." My brother whined.

"Awwww my poor baby." she replied, making a pouty face. "I have some Tylenol in the bathroom cabinet."

She took my brother under her arm and led him away. I began to make my way downstairs to my bedroom when I felt her attention turn to me.

"Don't get too far. We're having family fun night." She said this while shooting daggers at me with her eyes."

That's ridiculous. I thought. *We've never done anything like that before.* Nevertheless, I remained silent and took a seat at the kitchen table. My brother who was tasked with picking out the game returned with Jenga as Tom came home from work. The three of them gathered around me and set up the tower. Every piece that came out caused the three of them to erupt into a fit of the most riotous fake laughter I have ever had the misfortune of hearing. They were trying to convince themselves that they were having fun, and I hated them for it.

Is it really that difficult to be authentic? I thought.

It was my turn and they all turned their attention to me.

"You're always so moody." Jeannie said, mocking me with a frowny face.

"Yeah, just cheer up and have some fun." Tom added.

My blood was boiling. The fact that they were angry at me for quitting school didn't bother me, but the fact that they hid that anger behind a phony mirthful exterior filled me with an uncontrollable rage.

I snapped. "I'm not just going to sit here and pretend like everything's ok when it isn't."

"What are you talking about?" Tom said. "No one is attacking you."

Classic minimization, I thought, the psychological phenomenon where an abuser denies abuse has occurred or insists it was just a joke.

I got up to leave, but my brother cried out "You can't leave. The game isn't over yet and it's your turn!"

I turned around and swung my fist as hard as I could at the Jenga tower sending the pieces flying across the room. "Oops. I guess I lost." I said and stormed back outside to my car.

When I got outside, I noticed that the weather had worsened, but I didn't care. I just had to get away from the house and be alone. Still, the roads were in no condition to be driven upon so I parked in the McDonald's parking lot and smoked several cigarettes back to back. My thoughts began to race.

Where was family fun night when I was a teenager who spent all of my time alone in my room playing World of Warcraft? They didn't want a relationship with me then, and now they set up a situation that they could repeat to anyone else as evidence of their cruel treatment at the hands of their son. I could just hear Jeannie say, her face covered in the fakest of tears "I just wanted to spend time with my family, but Christopher ruined everything for no reason." Her friends would then comfort her and tell her she was a good mother, but they would never know about when I was a child and terrified in the middle of the night because I saw aliens outside of my window and I went to my mother to feel safe she would tell me to go back to bed and so I would go back to my room and hide under the covers night after night.

Fuck her I thought, and I worked myself up even more by repeating those same thoughts over and over again for hours, but then I thought about something else. Jeannie surely didn't even have the self awareness to realize that the way she treated me was unhealthy. It's not like she even had the faintest idea of what attachment theory was. She mocked me because her mother had mocked her who mocked her because she had been mocked herself. It was a shitty situation all around, but I couldn't be mad anymore because there was no one to be mad at - It was just the way things were, and so I inadvertently stumbled into a state of Quiet Resignation and fell asleep right there in the McDonald's parking lot.

I spent the rest of break in my room with the exception of Thanksgiving and the following day where I went along with Tom, Jeannie, and my brother to visit Jeannie's family. They lived about four hours away, and I only ever saw them at Christmas and Thanksgiving. Jeannie always talked like I was supposed to feel something for them, but I don't see how I could be expected to. You just never get close to people if you only see them for a few hours every year.

It was just Jeannie's mother and sister who were left. Everyone else had died. Someone died when I was in Kindergarten. Someone died when I was in first grade. Someone died when I was in second grade, and so on until I had accepted it as a fact of life that precisely one person in your family will die each year.

When we arrived at Jeannie's mother's, we seated ourselves in the living room and proceeded to have a conversation. When it was time for Jeannie's mother to acknowledge me, she turned and asked me how school was going. I told her I quit.

She gasped and turned to Jeannie "How could you let him do this?" scolding her.

Jeannie remained silent and looked at the ground.

Jeannie's mother turned back to me and exclaimed "But that's not like you at all!"

I wondered to myself how she felt comfortable making that judgement when she didn't seem to have any real conception as to what I might actually be like in the first place. I just stood up and went downstairs to the basement to watch the shitty television that my brother and I always watched when we were at her house. I had no intention of sitting there and being made to feel guilty. I didn't feel guilty at all, and as I left I thought I saw a small glimmer of pride in Tom's eyes but I wasn't really sure.

A while later my brother joined me in the basement and asked "How could you be so rude to sweet old Grandma?"

I ignored him and focused intently on the show about misbehaving dogs. The British woman who came into people's homes to train their dogs was rather attractive.

At Thanksgiving dinner that night people's attitudes towards me started to change. They talked to me more like an equal. I liked that. They all wondered if I had a girlfriend. I said yes and talked about Reanne like she was my girlfriend. Of course I hadn't seen her for almost two months, but in my mind she was my girlfriend.

The next day, everything on television was about Black Friday. Apparently half a dozen people had died across the country because they had been trampled to death by people scrambling to get the best deal on a flat screened TV or a blender or something. It made me sick to think of people as the animals they clearly were so I turned off the television and stared at the wall until it was time to go back to Tom and Jeannie's house. I intended to head back to Iowa State as soon as I got there. I had had enough of everyone.

When Tom said goodbye he asked what my future plans were, but I ignored him because I knew he would shit all over anything I had to say. I thought about Howard Hughes. Maybe the biggest factor in his success was the fact that his father was dead by the time he was twenty. It's hard for me to believe that Howard could have approached his father with the idea to use their fortune to make movies and be met with any response other than "Are you out of your damn mind? What the hell do you know about making movies?"

When Jeannie said goodbye she told me that there was still time for me to change my mind and stay in school. I simply pitied her for being so small-minded so as to think that I was doomed to a life of complete and utter failure without a college degree. Then again, most people think that because that's what everyone else thinks. Most people never think for themselves. In fact, I am apt to wonder if whether or not one can even think original thoughts without a degree of psychopathy in their character. Without it, one's actions are entirely governed by the social norms in a particular setting and the power structure that exists.

I truly am haunted by the results of Stanley Milgram's obedience experiment. I know I've already brought it up in this text, but I brood upon it endlessly. When Milgram first designed the experiment, he only expected one out of every two hundred people to obey the authority figure to the point of killing someone. The actual results were closer to two out of three. It's the "banality of evil". The worst atrocities are committed by ordinary people who feel they're not holding responsibility. Adolf Eichmann, the man who worked out all of the logistics for the Holocaust was found to be "a completely ordinary and average man" when subject to psychiatric evaluation.

For all the bad rap I get from people who say I'm a "bad person" because I'm selfish, manipulative, rude, or whatever, I know I wouldn't have the slightest discomfort telling the authority figure to "fuck off." In fact, I've only ever been in one fight during my life and that was to stop a bully from picking on a retarded kid.So what if I enjoyed slamming the bully's face into the pavement a little too much? The means were justified by the end.

But is this enough to make me a "good person"? I don't think it is even worth thinking about; there is only what happens to be. Since my behavior is solely the result of the particular brain chemistry I have, making a value judgement about it is pointless since simply calling it "good" or "bad" does absolutely nothing to change it. The dark triad of personality traits, narcissism, machiavellianism, and psychopathy evolved as an alternative fast-life strategy to reproduce early and often without sticking around to raise the children. If I could be any other way, I would, but I can't.

It's the same reason I am inclined to withdraw making the same sort of ethical judgements about other people. With a different brain chemistry I might be subject to the same sadistic impulse that makes people bullies, and another might see me so timid and wracked with fear that I would gladly comply with whatever the authority figure said so as to avoid the immense discomfort of interpersonal confrontation.

When I had arrived back at Iowa State, I was back to being on my own, and I found it to be a great relief. I spent my time walking, and as I walked, I repeated the same festering thoughts over and over again, spurred onward by my own grandiosity. As soon as the semester was over, I would move across the country and make a life for myself without anyone to hold me back. I would pull myself up by my bootstraps and become the living embodiment of both the American Dream and the quintessential Byronic hero.

After all? How could I possibly fail? Objectively I have all the qualities of a Great Man. Intelligence, physical beauty, ruthlessness, and a single mindedness to endlessly pursue that which I desire most. Yes, History was nothing more than the biography of Great Men as Herbert Spencer declared and it was clear to me that my biography and the fate of everyone else were one and the same.

As I was in the cafeteria, trapped in my mind and unable to think of anything else, I was heading towards a secluded spot near the window where I might sit down to eat when Reanne suddenly appeared in front of me. (One week had passed since Thanksgiving break.) Neither of us said anything, and we just stood there staring into each other's eyes unable to look away. Ecstasy and pleasure once more! Reanne started to giggle like a little girl and it occurred to me that she must be laughing at me because of how unusual it is to make eye contact like that without saying anything. I didn't want to look away, but we were starting to draw attention from the other students so I told her it was nice to see her and proceeded onward to my seat.

It's strange, usually everything around me seems dull and nothing holds my interest, but interacting with Reanne changes that for me. For a short time afterwards I feel myself drawn, as if pulled on by an invisible force to sounds, colors, and people whose qualities fill me with a lightness of being, a conscious enjoyment of being alive.

Presently, my focus was entirely on Reanne. I was no longer hungry. There she was, not more than thirty feet from me in the middle of a large table filled up with people (almost exclusively guys), and she was the utter center of attention. She stood up and arched her back slightly which was very attractive. It occurred to me that she must be ovulating considering how flirtatious she was being. I watched her walk over to a rather effeminate looking boy at the end of the table and put her finger under his chin. The boy's face was bright red and he was looking down at the ground, but Reanne just kept staring at him with that characteristic malicious grin - big and goofy smile at the mouth but with the nose wrinkled a little bit and sparkling eyes that showed she was up to no good.

I laughed internally. Doubtlessly he was one of her evangelical friends. I imagine he was feeling shameful because of the desire Reanne had aroused in him, and I would really pity him if he ever attempted to act on it. Surely Reanne would react with nothing more than a scolding "How dare you! I'm not that kind of girl!" before storming off, leaving the boy alone and bashful, while she would hurry off to her room and vigorously finger herself to the memory.

I continued staring at Reanne, hoping she would return the glance and allow us to make eye contact again, but she avoided my gaze completely and I soon left the cafeteria.

Later that evening I received a text message from Reanne. It was a Bible passage, Psalm 145: 18-20 to be precise.

The Lord is near to all who call on him, to all who call on him in truth. He fulfills the desire of those who fear him; he also hears their cry and saves them. The Lord preserves all who love Him, but all the wicked He will destroy.

I countered with Machiavelli.

Any man that tries to be good all the time will come to ruin among the vast number who are not good. Thus any man who wishes to maintain his authority must learn how not to be good and judiciously be good or not good as the situation demands.

She parried with Galatians 6:9.

Let us not grow weary of doing good for at the proper time we will reap a harvest if we do not give up.

I responded with my own voice.

The problem with quoting scripture in a clash of wits is the fact that scripture is only an authority if I choose to regard it as such and submit myself to its influence.

She did not respond to me that night, but the next day I heard back from her.

Whatever. I just thought you just looked upset when I saw you yesterday and I wanted to give you some encouragement. I hope you're well.

Reading the message filled me with anxiety. I could not reconcile the tender side of Reanne and her affectionate emotions with the animal I knew her to be - a biological machine merely avoiding negative stimuli and seeking positive ones. I froze up for a while until the emotion became unbearable and I had no other want than a singular desire to connect with Reanne.

I apologize for not treating you as an equal. That's all I said.

She responded immediately.

I'm sorry for ignoring you.

At that moment, for all of the misunderstanding that had happened between us, I felt united with her. I was struck by an arousal the likes of which I had never experienced before. There was nothing else I wanted out of life than to be inside of her. I would have been, I know it, if she was anywhere within my general proximity, but she wasn't and we were communicating by text message.

Meet up? I asked.

She didn't respond for twenty minutes. The urge had all but faded by then.

I honestly don't think that's a good idea.

I wasn't angry. I could sense that she was actually being genuine. The fact that she took so long to respond made it clear that she was wrestling internally with the cognitive dissonance caused by her own arousal and her commitment to wait until marriage. I felt like Zarathustra when he first comes down from the mountain and sees the saint whistling in the woods. He has no desire to take that away from the poor man, and so he thinks to himself: *That poor soul, he has not yet heard the news. He has not yet heard that God is dead.* And so he carries on upon his way.

A few hours passed and I reached out again.

I would like to spend time with you. I do not plan on returning to Iowa State next semester.

Reanne did not respond again and any other messages I sent were blocked.

Part 4

During the last few weeks of the fall semester, I was endlessly frustrated. Reanne had finally begun to fade from mind, only to rush back in and dominate my thoughts. I couldn't sleep for several nights, and the stress inside of me continued to build to the point that it severely affected my cognitions and behavior. People would pass me and wish me good day and I would inadvertently snap and speak with an aggressive tone and posture when I attempted to reciprocate in kind.

Hoping to distract myself, I returned to my speech communication course for the first time since the beginning of the semester. When I entered, the other students briefly turned to me and with a confused expression quickly formed their judgements. I was flunking out, that much was obvious to them, but the way they lept from that fact to a nonverbal expression about my character really rubbed me the wrong way.

I took an empty seat in the middle of the classroom while they returned to conversing with their various social groups they had formed over the course of the semester. I was wearing all black, so of course I did not fit in with any of them. The way they joked and laughed amongst themselves, referencing the latest Marvel movie that came out over the weekend made me feel as if I had nothing in common with any of them. I wanted to bang my head against the desk.

Obviously I didn't make any effort to converse with them. I just sat there and thought about how much I disliked superhero movies. They were all the same with their car chases and fights on top of moving trains. In fact, I couldn't understand how anyone could enjoy them at all, but I watched the other students out of the corner of my eye and then it made sense to me. They were all the same too in their Iowa State hoodies. I disliked them all, but I could tell that the way I was able to sit there alone but completely comfortable in my own skin unnerved them a bit but also caused them to be a bit in awe of me too. I liked that.

I was just imagining going to the movies with Reanne when that same pudgy TA with the wrinkled shirt walked in and announced that we would be giving improvisational speeches today. Each of us would be assigned a topic and after receiving two minutes to prepare we would then give our speech to the class, taking extra care, of course, to showcase the techniques we learned over the course of the semester (he looked directly at me when he said this last part).

As the class went on, I watched the other students both when they spoke and how they listened (or rather stared blankly off into space bored out of their minds with the canned speeches) when they were in the audience. I watched the TA and noticed how self-satisfied he looked as he continuously marked "needs improvement" on the rubrics.

"How many of you guys like pizza?" That was how one student started his speech, utilizing the technique of starting your speech by asking a question.

"Knock Knock. Who's there?" That was how another student started his speech. He was trying to start a speech by using humor.

I felt the rage and disgust building within me. Could you imagine Pericles or Adolf Hitler starting a speech with a knock knock joke as a ham-fisted attempt to create a catchy "attention grabber"? It was ludicrous.

When it was my turn to go, I received the topic for my speech.

Please give an instructional speech on the proper technique for licking an ice cream cone.

I sat there in the planning area and imagined myself giving the speech like I was supposed to. Making a fool out of myself by talking about ice cream through gritted teeth as if it were a serious scholarly question to a group of my peers not listening to a single word only to receive a bad grade anyway for "lacking the proper enthusiasm". Internally I snapped and screamed *THIS IS ALL HORSESHIT*, but I looked around and noticed my peers were all looking at me with eager anticipation. Whereas they had all spent their two minutes of preparation nervously jotting down notes, I was sitting there as outwardly calm and collected as always with my legs crossed and a finger on my chin, deep in thought, and paying no worry at all to whatever grade the TA decided to give me.

Perhaps I can give a good speech after all, I thought to myself and smirked as I strolled casually up to the front of the classroom.

For the first time in my life, the enthralled attention of my peers brought life and voice to my innermost reflections.

"I received for my topic 'How to lick an ice cream cone'." I paused and looked around the room. "But I will not speak to you today on that subject for the simple reason that it does not interest me in the slightest. In fact, I believe that the sole requirement for giving a good speech is to be so utterly convinced that what you are speaking is the truth that you are naturally emphatic enough with your words and expressions that it becomes impossible for your audience to escape from the contagion of your mood.

In seeking that aim today, I will speak to you instead regarding the singular object occupying my mind, and I have no doubt that you, my dear audience, will be able to relate entirely with what I have to say. I am speaking, of course, with reference to the most human of experiences, Romantic Love, and I declare it to be the most human of experiences because at the end of the day we are, all of us, nothing more than mammals who live our lives seeking to reproduce and pass on our genes to the next generation.

Have you ever met someone and you could not, and I mean COULD NOT, despite all of your willful efforts shake the person from your mind? The reason for this rather annoying predicament is that the levels of serotonin in your brain actually drop to the same level as that found in people who suffer from chronic OCD.

Indeed, through no moral fault of your own, you may find yourself so single-mindedly obsessed with another person that you become entirely unable to function in society, and any possibility of leading the normal life expected of you is gone.

When Darwin had developed his theory of natural selection, he reflected with horror upon the parasitic wasp that laid its eggs within the body of a living caterpillar. As the eggs hatched and the larvae grew, they consumed the caterpillar from within, causing it to suffer excruciating pain. What horrified Darwin the most was that this seemingly senseless display of brutality wasn't senseless at all, but the logical conclusion of the natural order of life. The parasitic wasp evolved because the reproductive strategy it employed worked entirely indifferent to the sufferings it imposed upon the caterpillar.

We, humans, likewise evolved in the same harsh and indifferent environment and the reproductive strategies our biology employs is likewise entirely indifferent to the suffering it inflicts upon others. Now, I do not mean to say that the experience of Romantic Love is not enjoyable. That is certainly not the case, for Romantic Love is doubtlessly the most pleasurable experience I've ever had, but the pleasure, which is a release of dopamine, is deceptive in the same way that a poisonous berry might taste sweet, for the reproductive strategies of males and females are so at odds with one another that pain is the inevitable result.

Males are subject to the Coolidge effect, rendering them liable to become sexually bored with any long term partner, while women are predisposed to seek out a more masculine man than their long term partner while they're ovulating. It's horse shit all around, and enough to make you sick to your stomach, but the really fucked up thing is that there's no way out and there's no one to blame.

Even if I'm completely aware that women are just creatures who are perfectly evolved to emotionally ensnare me so that I'll provide resources for them and their offspring, a woman smiles at me and my serotonin drops all the same and I'll throw everything away to be with her, and as angry as it makes me I can't be angry at her anymore than I can be angry at the parasitic wasp. It's just the way things are.

But what I do hate is the moral condemnation of everyone who isn't self aware enough to know that things can't be anyway other than the way things are."

At this point I was overcome with emotion and burst into tears.

"I just hate how everyone thinks I'm an asshole when I'm just in love, but too scared to do anything about it."

After that I walked out of the room so I could have a good cry undisturbed in the bathroom. After I had spent a few minutes sobbing uncontrollably like a baby, I began to feel better. I started laughing to myself and I wondered if my tears were real in the first place or just a theatrical display. I still don't really know the truth to be honest.

Once I could think clearly again, I reflected on the stunned faces I noticed as I calmly walked out of the classroom. The TA had his face down, red with embarrassment, while all the girls were playing with their hair and had expressions on their faces that indicated that they were currently creaming their pants. I didn't pay any attention to how any of the guys reacted to my speech, but I concluded that I had ended up giving a pretty good speech solely because I had been genuine, and felt satisfied with myself that my time at Iowa State hadn't been a complete waste.

I called up Fabian and asked if he wanted to have dinner at the Chinese restaurant.

He told me when he picked up. "You know you're the only person who ever calls people anymore, right? It's kind of weird."

I replied, annoyed. "Are you coming or not?"

He responded. "Yeah sure, I'll meet you there in twenty minutes."

After I recounted the story of the speech to him, he laughed and said. "You know they all thought you were completely insane, right?"

I laughed and replied. "Maybe they thought I was a genius."

He laughed louder. He was an excitable person and had a habit of laughing progressively louder. "No," he said "They thought you were insane. I guarantee it."

"Maybe you're right," I said without laughing "But if I ever end up making any sort of name for myself they'll all brag at dinner parties that they knew I was a genius all along."

"You might be right about that," he said without laughing "but on that same note if you ever end up starting a cult or murdering somebody or something they'll tell the story and mention how they knew you were completely nuts from the moment they first saw you."

"You're probably right about that," I agreed, laughing, and seeing some truth in what he had to say.

We finished eating in pensive silence until I broke it.

"Fabian," I said. "I'm glad you're my friend."

Fabian laughed a bit before saying "I'm glad you're my friend too, bud." but he didn't make eye contact when he said it. I'm not entirely sure what that indicates.

On one of my last days at Iowa State I was walking when I saw Reanne off in the distance walking towards my direction. I stopped and waited for her to catch up and her face lit up when she saw me. She asked why I was leaving school, and the way she looked up at me made her seem to me an innocent little girl. I didn't answer her. I just stared at the faint moustache above her upper lip and focused on the complete and utter revulsion I felt towards it.

"But how can you leave school? You're so smart!" She said, even sounding like a little girl.

I walked away from her and shortly after received a text message.

Whatever happens, I wish you the absolute best in your future endeavors.

I read through it twice, but I didn't respond right away. I felt ashamed, I don't know how else to put it. Ashamed at everything I'd done.

Later on I sent her a naked picture so she'd have something to remember me by, I lifted for her sake, after all.

I packed up everything in my apartment and returned to Tom and Jeannie's house. I had this idea in my head to move someplace far away and set up a way of getting passive income through bonds or real estate or something so I could spend my time walking around a big city, but Tom, who had always told me the money he saved through my full ride scholarship would be given to me, said he didn't feel comfortable giving me the money with my current mental state. It seemed like a reasonable response from his outside point of view, so I didn't argue with him.

I got sucked into World of Warcraft for the next few months (the game does a great job of stimulating the goal-reward motivators of human behavior) and didn't really do anything until I wanted something different so I took a job at a fast food restaurant. It was a thoroughly novel experience to be around other people after a period of such social isolation. It was as if the very experience of my consciousness had changed and I was no longer an outside observer, but instead an active participant in the life around me. I flirted innocently with the girls and I played basketball with my coworkers on our days off. I started spending a lot of time with Michael and we attended lots of parties around town. Life was fun, plain and simple, but I still could not escape the knowledge that positive emotions evolved to facilitate social bonding. Do you ever find yourself talking to someone and you can't understand what they're saying but you still enjoy interacting with them nonetheless?

At this point in the story, I have a confession to make. I have not been entirely truthful with you, my dear reader, for I was at this time still a virgin. I know I have claimed to bed several women so far, but though I can assure you that the sexual tension was real in each of those instances, I nevertheless failed to ever consummate it for the simple fact that it always occurred in a public place or at some other inopportune time.

I did, however, during this time create an account on tinder, and though I have several hundred matches and enjoy the validation it gives me, I never end up meeting with any of them. It reminds me once more of Kierkegaard. I paraphrase:

If there's a girl who has caught my eye and sent me madly to the state of obsessive love, it would never occur to me that I might fail to win her affection, and for that reason I always succeed. It's finding a girl that's worth pursuing that's the hard part.

I guess I just lied to you, my dear reader, because I was insecure and I didn't want you to think I was some sort of failure as a man. For that, you have my deepest, sincerest apologies.

This time period was also refreshing, because the ability to mingle with people who had no preconceived notions of who I was allowed me to reinvent myself and unlock the hidden charisma within my character. I came up with a party game that involved locking eye contact and tossing a lighter back and forth using only one's peripheral vision. I knew it would work to break the ice because prolonged eye contact releases oxytocin which is responsible for the feeling of trust.

It seemed harmless at first. I would walk into a party and smile to myself as I overheard people ask "Whoa, who is that guy?" I felt invincible, and at the end of every night there would be a group of people gathered around me looking at me with complete and utter deference and devotion.

Then strange things started to happen that filled me with abject terror. The interpersonal attraction was so strong that the others seemed to spiral inwards toward me. I understand why a cult leader might say "We are all the same person", it certainly seemed like it. The other people seemed to to exist merely as extensions of my own will. Luckily I was aware that what we we were experiencing was just symptom of crowd psychology where the individual identity is lost within the identity of the group. If I actually would have said we were the same person, I think they would have believed me and we would have started a cult right then and there.

The final straw occurred one night when we were out walking on the street and there was a man walking in the opposite direction. I was overwhelmed with the impulse to beat the man to death for no reason at all. I resisted it, of course, but knowing that the impulse was there and that other people would have joined me horrified me to the core. My whole adolescence I dreamed of power, but now I wanted nothing to do with it.

We returned to someone's house and we were all in a circle facing each other. We were all very excited and moving closer together until we had a collective realisation that we were about half a second away from breaking out into a massive orgy. That's when something inside of me snapped and I started seeing visions of the future.

I was the next Adolf Hitler. I was the next Jim Jones. I was the next Ted Bundy. I saw people on their knees worshiping me and I knew it could actually happen. When Jesus told people to drop everything and follow him, they actually did. That's the crazy thing about charisma. If I started telling people I was Jesus they might actually believe me. I understood it completely.

I couldn't live like that; I care too much about my legacy to be remembered as a petty charleton and rake. I broke the spell and walked out.

I had to get away from everybody. I heard people behind me talking about me in code. I heard one guy say.

"Holy shit. I think he actually turned me gay for a minute."

They were about to call the police on me and so I quickly got into my car and drove back to Tom and Jeannie's house. I was pretty shaken up for a while after that. I kept thinking more about Stanley Milgram's obedience experiment. I was the authority figure, but I was so unfit to be the authority figure. My sadism, my racism, my ruthlessness, my lust all shaped by Nature to dominate. I am the parasitic wasp. The difference is, I'm aware of being a parasitic wasp. But what is a parasitic wasp to do once it becomes aware of its own nature but is entirely unable to change it?

Obviously suicide is the completely ethical answer, but I didn't really want to kill myself. Instead I withdrew completely from society. I quit my job and severed all relationships without any explanation. I live in Tom and Jeannie's basement. I don't speak to them much. I stay up until 5:00 AM and sleep until 3:00 PM. I have a whiteboard in my room covered with phrases that seemed poetical to me - pathological ineptitude, maladaptive discontent, the virtuous estrangement. There's some differential equations too.

I post a lot on 4chan. Between all of the shitposting and calling everyone cucks there's actually some pretty insightful conversation the likes of which you'd never find anywhere where the identities aren't anonymous.

Occasionally, I look up Reanne's Instagram. She's in the Caribbean on a boat doing some missionary work through a program called Seaway 2 Salvation. I even still send her a text from time to time even though I know she won't respond. I have no future now, and so my utility is gone for her.

I live isolated. I am a parasitic wasp that has sworn off its sustenance, succeeding, but actively working against the flourishing of its own life.

Still, there is a hope that remains in the back of my mind. If the outside world ever finds itself thrown into chaos, I could be useful. I could bring order. It could happen. I read that 65% of people in my generation do not identify as capitalists.God must have had some reason for creating the parasitic wasp, after all. That's what I tell myself anyway.

I want to smoke, but I don't want to hear Jeannie's passive aggressive comments so I sneak out the back staircase.

And here I am, searching for Orion in the night sky, but I don't see Orion. Instead I see only the stars and the shapes they form themselves into within my own perception: first a cat, then a cowboy hat, a gardening trowel, and an automobile.

I feel that my entire existence rests on the very edge of sanity. People either react like I've said something profound or complete gibberish everytime I open my mouth. I seriously fear ending up in a mental institution. Am I still insane if I'm aware of my insanity?

I'm so disinhibited. I feel like I'm sitting in the backseat of my own life and there's no breaks on the car. My self control is so poor I feel like I can't be around people because I'm not sure what's going to happen. Pascal said that all of humanity's problems come from its inability to sit in a room quietly by itself. Luckily I can do that.

Now I read Max Stirner and I know what I am. I am *The Creative Nothing*. Morality's a *spook*. Achievement's a *spook*. Religion's a *spook* and nationalism is too. Everything, including you, my dear reader, is my property. I merely have yet to obtain power over it. But the thing is, I don't really want to.

"I have never been joyful, and yet it has always seemed as if joy were my constant companion, as if the buoyant jinn of joy danced around me, invisible to others but not to me, whose eyes shone with delight. Then when I walk past people, happy-go-lucky as a god, and they envy me because of my good fortune, I laugh, for I despise people, and I take my revenge. I have never wished to do anyone an injustice, but I have always made it appear as if anyone who came close to me would be wronged and injured. Then when I hear others praised for their faithfulness, their integrity, I laugh, for I despise people, and I take my revenge. My heart has never been hardened toward anyone, but I have always made it appear, especially when I was touched most deeply, as if my heart were closed and alien to every feeling. Then when I hear others lauded for their good hearts, see them loved for their deep, rich feelings, then I laugh, for I despise people and take my revenge. When I see myself cursed, abhorred, hated for my coldness and heartlessness, then I laugh, then my rage is satisfied. The point is that if the good people could make me actually be in the wrong, make me actually do an injustice-well, then I would have lost." - Soren Kierkegaard

www.ingramcontent.com/pod-product-compliance
Lightning Source LLC
Chambersburg PA
CBHW070114290526
45789CB00005B/2024